BACKCOUNTRY
COOKING

BACKCOUNTRY
COOKING

FROM PACK
TO PLATE
IN 10 MINUTES

Dorcas S. Miller

BACKPACKER
THE MAGAZINE OF WILDERNESS TRAVEL

Published by
The Mountaineers
1001 SW Klickitat Way, Suite 201
Seattle, WA 98134

BACKPACKER
THE MAGAZINE OF WILDERNESS TRAVEL

33 East Minor Street
Emmaus, PA 18098

First edition, 1998

Published simultaneously in Great Britain by Cordee, 3a DeMontfort Street, Leicester, England, LE1 7HD

Printed in Canada

Edited by Cynthia Newman Bohn
All photographs by the author unless otherwise noted.
Cover design by Helen Cherullo
Book design and layout by Alice C. Merrill

Cover photograph: *Sunrise at 2800 meters in Minami Alps National Park, South Alps, Chubu Region, Japan* © Patrick Morrow

Library of Congress Cataloging-in-Publication Data

Miller, Dorcas S., 1949–
    Backcountry cooking : from pack to plate in 10 minutes / Dorcas Miller. — 1st ed.
       p.   cm.
    ISBN 0-89886-551-4
    1. Outdoor cookery. 2. Quick and easy cookery. 3. Camping—Equipment and supplies. I. Title.
    TX823.M526 1998
    641.5'78—dc21   97-50341
                                                         CIP

Table of Contents

Introduction

I've often heard outdoorspeople say, "I lived on ramen noodles" or "I ate instant oatmeal for breakfast and a box of macaroni and cheese every night." Filling and inexpensive, but dull. There are also folks who rely on freeze-dried meals. Convenient but expensive. The irony is that it is possible to make meals that are not only delicious but quick and simple to fix on trail.

This book is about how to do just that. Chapter 1 looks at the wide range of ingredients that are now available and suggests how to stock your backcountry cupboard. (Yes, it is useful to browse through Chapter 1 before you launch into the recipes.) Chapter 2 gives tips on low-fuel cooking, dehydrating food at home, baking on trail, keeping a Leave No Trace backcountry kitchen, and forestalling problems with critters.

With meals that are quick and easy to prepare, you can spend less time in the backcountry kitchen and more time relaxing.

The "Read This First" information that precedes the recipes (see page 43) is a must-read. This brief section provides information that is critical to using the no-cook recipes, explains the nutritional information listed at the end of each recipe, and includes instructions for making substitutions and enlarging recipes. Chapters 3 through 7 are stocked with recipes to tickle your taste buds and warm your heart. Some of the recipes are as easy as adding boiling water. Others, like pizza, require patience but reward you handsomely.

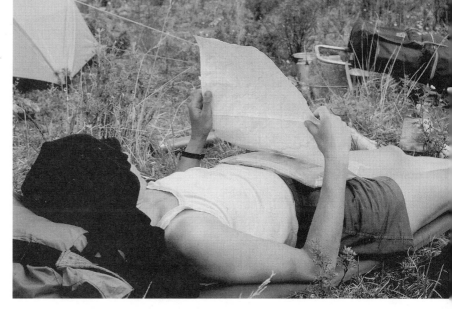

What Kind of Cook are You?

An Ascetic: You go in for minimal prep and minimal cooking—energy bars, PB&J, and boiling water for freeze-dried meals.

A Pragmatist: You carry one or two pots, use those handy supermarket packages of Chinese noodles and pasta with sauce (or equivalents), and have developed your own formula for efficient eating.

A Gourmand: You take a full-scale cook kit and plan food for its pleasure, flavor, and variety; you enjoy the process of cooking and food is a critical part of the trip for you.

The benefit of putting together your own meals, instant or not, is that you get to eat what *you* want to eat, not what someone else has decided to sell. You can include your own particular comfort foods (chocolate, java, Earl Grey tea, mashed potatoes, hard candy, miso, or whatever makes you feel snug and secure). You can decide the amount you'll eat, rather than having to adjust to what the package offers, and you can use the nutritional information included with each recipe to make sure you get enough calories. And, for those who see meals as a social occasion—a time to share insights and laughs about the day—there are great opportunities for putting on a real spread.

Whether you classify yourself as an ascetic, a pragmatist, or a gourmand reveals a lot about your take on food, as I discovered when I invited trail veterans to share their insights on cooking in the backcountry. I asked long-time trail denizens about their approach to food, their favorite meals, and their hard-won tips for the trail kitchen. I also asked food providers about their views on backcountry trends and the challenges they deal with daily when providing food for hungry outdoorspeople. The shrewd, funny, and enlightening responses from these trail-wise cooks appear as "Hot Tips" scattered throughout the chapters.

As for backcountry style, it seems fair that I answer that question myself. I'm a combination pragmatist and gourmand. I'm willing to put in time at home to dry food and assemble ingredients, so that when I'm on trail I don't have to fuss. When I go out with my husband, Ben, we eat very simply—hot or cold cereal and bagels for breakfast, an array of snacks for lunch, a one-pot meal for dinner, and sometimes something sweet for dessert. On trips with other people, though, I plan a basic rotation of dishes and garnish it liberally with special touches.

My favorite recipes? For breakfast, Apricot-Pecan Cream Cereal and Hash Browns with Scrambled Eggs. For lunch, I'm partial to having lots of options: nuts, dried fruit, a carbo (bagel, flatbread, or crackers), a spread, cheese, pretzels, fruit snack bars, homemade jerky, and maybe something off-beat like dulse (a seaweed). Pemmican Soup, Corn Chowder, and Hot Almond Smoothies are great side dishes. I like too many of the dinners to choose, though I do lean toward Crustless Russian Vegetable Pie and the wraps. For desserts, Mincemeat Pudding and Coconut-Mango Rice Pudding are super easy (and super tasty), Some More S'mores are decadent, and the boil-in-a-bag recipes are fun.

As for favorite gadgets, I prize my dehydrator at home and my insulated bowl and mug on trail.

PART I

SKILLS FOR BACKCOUNTRY COOKING

CHAPTER 1

Know Your Ingredients

For food we had flour, beans, bacon, tea, coffee, sugar, condensed milk, rolled oats, butter, dried fruit, sweet choco-late, beef extract, rice, and desiccated potatoes. To cook with we had brought two small alcohol stoves and two gallons of denatured alcohol. Emergency rations and the like were not obtainable. . . . On taking to the glacier, we had dispatched two men to Mr. Barrett's cache for a Yukon stove, and the next day made use of the last fuel we should find, the small willows about us, to bake [fifteen pans of] biscuits and boil [twenty-five pounds of] beans for the entire trip.

Dora Keen, "Mountain Climbing in Alaska:
The First Expedition to Mount Blackburn," *Appalachia,* 1912

Just as siting your tent is "location, location, location," preparing backcountry meals is "ingredients, ingredients, ingredients." Find-ing ingredients is much easier than it used to be because supermarkets are carrying more products that are uniquely suited for trail life—products such as couscous, bulgur, instant refried beans, dried hummus, instant hash browns, precooked bacon, and all types of dried fruit and vegetables.

If you are willing to order food by mail or visit your local Asian market and health food stores, the options multiply quickly. You can get freeze-dried and dehydrated vegetables, freeze-dried meat, and lots of unusual ingredients, such as coconut cream powder and blue cheese powder, to add zest to backcountry eating. Mail order is, after all, only a phone call away.

This chapter presents information about ingredients that are used later in the recipes. For where to find these ingredients, please see Appendix A.

GRAINS AND GRAIN PRODUCTS

Bulgur is wheat that has been cracked, steamed, and dried. Commonly used in Middle Eastern dishes, it has come into its own in the United States as a convenience food in the form of wheat pilaf. Bulgur comes in three sizes—largest for pilaf, mid-sized for cereal, and smallest for tabouli. Buy the smallest grain for instant meals and use the mid-sized and large grain in recipes that call for simmering or overnight soaking.

Couscous is wheat or millet that has been cracked, steamed, and dried. It is usually white, though several companies market brown (whole wheat) couscous. This versatile food comes to us from North Africa, where it is a staple. Its small size allows it to rehydrate quickly in no-cook recipes.

Instant grits are grits (granular pieces of hulled corn from which the germ has been removed) that have been cooked and dried. They are about the same size as grains of couscous. Instant grits are sold packaged in individual portions (use two per person) or in a box with a pour spout.

Oat flakes or rolled oats are oats that have undergone processing that includes removing the hull, rolling the groats, then steaming and drying the resulting flakes. Thin oat flakes cook faster than thick ones.

Quick or one-minute oats are oats that need to be simmered in water for one minute to make oatmeal.

Instant oats, available in boxes or single-serving packages, require only the addition of boiling water to make oatmeal.

Instant rice, or one-minute rice, is a common ingredient in backcountry food bags. Add boiling water, let the rice stand 10 minutes, and you have a cup of rice. Instant rice is available in white and brown forms. I prefer white, which has better flavor and texture. Instant rice of any kind is highly processed, so the brown variety won't have all the vitamins and minerals found in regular brown rice.

Freeze-dried brown rice retains some texture when reconstituted. It works in no-cook dishes and can be rehydrated between breakfast and lunch for a cold salad.

Basmati rice is used regularly in Indian food. If you are willing to take along rice that needs to be cooked, then this is a good choice because it requires only 10 to 15 minutes of simmering, rather than the 25 to 40 minutes required for some other types of rice.

Freeze-dried or quick-cooking wild rice. Sure, it's expensive, but

Fast-cooking ingredients make for quick meals in the mountains.

wild rice has a great nutty flavor that's even better on trail than it is at home. Freeze-dried rice will "cook" with the addition of boiling water. The quick-cook kind may take up to 7 minutes.

Roasted rice for beverages is rice that has been processed so that it rehydrates easily in tea or soup. You can find it in Asian food stores. While roasted rice can help give body to a soup, it has little texture of its own so it does not work well in a one-pot meal where texture is important.

Rice flakes are grains of cooked rice that have been squashed flat; they will "cook" with the addition of boiling water. Like roasted rice, they do not have a firm texture, and I have not called for their use in recipes.

Creamed rice, which is generally used as a hot cereal, is white rice that has been granulated.

Bread bases are wheat flour to which other ingredients have been added to create a new and different flavor. Options include spinach and feta base (dried spinach, grated feta cheese, onion, parsley, and basil) and black olive base (dried black olives, oregano, and garlic) among others. You can make your own bread bases by adding dried ingredients or purchase bases from gourmet food companies.

PASTA AND NOODLES

Chinese (instant ramen) noodles have been precooked and dried. This ingredient has become a mainstay of outdoor adventurers. Most meal-sized packages of ramen noodles come with a seasoning packet that is heavy on salt and monosodium glutamate. Even if you do not have to restrict your salt intake or are not allergic to MSG, you may want to use only part of the packet. As an alternative, look for Chinese noodles (or curly Japanese noodles) without seasoning packets in the Asian food section of your grocery store. In the recipes, I measure Chinese noodles by the cup, but if you have a scale handy, 1 ounce equals about ½ cup.

Pasta is usually made from wheat, though increasingly other ingredients—including spinach, tomato, mushrooms, chilis, lemon, and even smoked salmon—are being folded in. Pasta comes in dozens of shapes, from tiny stars that cook in a few minutes to larger tubes, spirals, and strips that take 8 to 10 or 11 minutes. Shells and rotini are convenient because you can eat them with a spoon. Spaghetti, a traditional favorite, is a challenge to manage even when broken into pieces. It is worth experimenting with different shapes, colors, and flavors to add welcome variety to your meals.

The chief drawback to pasta is that, in most recipes, you're instructed to heat a large pot of water, cook the pasta, and then drain off the water. A lot of gas is used to heat a lot of water that is then thrown away—a fairly inefficient process. In contrast, with grain-based meals all of the water heated is consumed.

No-cook (no-boil) pasta is available through mail order. Just add a small amount of boiling water and let the pasta stand—but don't throw away the water that is not absorbed. Dried vegetables and seasonings can turn the unused water into a savory broth that will help you stay hydrated.

Egg noodles come in several sizes, from thin, narrow noodles that cook in about 4 minutes to wider noodles that cook in 7 to 9 minutes. The smallest size, with noodles about 1½ inches long, works well with a bowl and spoon; you don't have to slurp as you do with spaghetti.

POTATOES

Freeze-dried potatoes are useful because they are quick-cooking, but they taste like and have the consistency of instant potatoes. With some doctoring, they can be used in hash browns, and their lack of texture is masked somewhat when they are used with other ingredients in a stew or one-pot meal.

Potato starch is a thickener that can be used in soups, smoothies, sauces, and desserts.

Instant hash browns are a boon for backcountry campers because crispy, golden hash browns are so wonderful and because whole potatoes are so heavy. There are other dehydrated potato products, including julienne potatoes and scalloped potatoes, both of which take about 15 minutes to rehydrate and cook. To make sure you buy instant hash browns, check the directions. They should tell you to add boiling water to the spuds, rather than directing you to simmer them. Instant hash brown mixes include dried onion flakes and other seasonings, so they're all set to go.

Instant mashed potatoes or potato flakes are a great base upon which to build a meal. By themselves, they have that "instant potato" taste and texture, which some people find more objectionable than others. Instant potatoes can be improved with seasoning and a dab of margarine or a teaspoon of butter powder.

BEANS AND OTHER LEGUMES

Instant refried beans and black bean powder greatly simplify Mexican cooking. Just add water and—presto!—you have seasoned refried beans, a key element in burritos, dips, and other dishes. These box mixes are widely available in supermarkets and health food stores.

Bean flakes come in several varieties (I've found black bean and pinto bean so far in various health food stores). The flakes contain salt but no other seasonings. Other than having to spice them up yourself, you can use them as you would the instant bean powder described above—just add boiling water and let the flakes stand for 5 minutes.

Freeze-dried beans and lentils are available through mail order. Choices include pinto, navy, black, and kidney beans plus lentils. In testing these foods (I added boiling water and let them stand for 10 minutes in an insulated mug), I found that some beans cooked/rehydrated all the way through while others retained a tiny powdery core. Those with the powdery core are edible, though they have an odd texture. When they're mixed with other ingredients, the texture problem is less noticeable.

Jean Spangenberg's Hot Tips

Jean is product development specialist at Adventure Foods, a family-owned business. She has written two cookbooks, *The BakePacker's Companion* and—with her husband, Sam—*The Portable Baker*. Jean is a consummate cook (see page 142 for her recipe for Bread Pudding).

Backcountry trends: (1) People want healthier foods—no additives, no preservatives. I've seen this trend growing over the last seven years. (2) People want to eat more like they would at home and are less willing to settle for canned foods, crackers, jerky, cheese, and gorp. Outdoorspeople still use these items but to a lesser degree than before.

Biggest challenges: It never ceases to amaze me that some outdoor enthusiasts think nothing of the money they put into buying equipment for their outdoor adventures, but when it comes to putting money into the necessary fuel (food) that keeps their most important piece of equipment (their bodies) going, they balk. Changing this perception of the importance of food is my biggest challenge.

The other big challenge is making sure people have the amount of food they need for a well-balanced diet, and making sure that the food offers enough variety to be enjoyable. Because people want food that tastes like homemade with little or no cooking—two fairly stiff criteria—our new products have evolved along those lines.

Trail wisdom: If you don't like an item well enough to eat it at home, don't take it on your trip.

Trail tip: To avoid carrying a container of oil, use mayonnaise portion packs for frying pancakes, eggs, tortillas, etc. The mayo melts right back down to the oil and does not give the food a mayonnaise flavor.

FRUITS AND VEGETABLES

Dried fruits of many kinds are available in supermarkets and specialty stores. Apples, apricots, pears, raisins, mangoes, papaya, cherries, pineapple, peaches, cranberries, blueberries—take your pick. The more exotic fruits may be expensive, but you only need a handful to get a delightful burst of flavor some afternoon when the miles are long and the pack is heavy.

Freeze-dried fruit, including blueberries, peaches, pineapple, and strawberries, is available through mail order. Freeze-dried blueberries look great, but no one is likely to mistake them for fresh. (But then, if you knew there were going to be fresh blueberries along the trail, you wouldn't take along their freeze-dried cousins.) The virtue of freeze-dried fruit is that it is extremely light and provides a taste of something that wouldn't otherwise be available. This type of fruit is best used in something, rather than by itself.

Orange powder gives a nice flavor to cereal, smoothies, and desserts. Orange-flavored breakfast drink, the taste of which I find somewhat artificial, can be substituted for orange powder. None of the recipes call for lemon powder because it is extremely strong and lemon flavor can be obtained from lemon zest.

Spiced cider dry mix can be used as a hot drink or added to desserts to provide extra flavor.

Coconut cream powder, found in Asian markets, is very rich and flavorful. Powdered coconut can be used as a substitute.

Dried vegetables, including carrots, bell peppers, cabbage, celery, corn, mushrooms, onions, tomatoes, and mixed veggies, are available in supermarkets and health food stores and through mail order. Before you bag up a big pile of instant meals, though, test a few pieces of each dried vegetable you plan to use to make sure that they will all rehydrate promptly (they should be ready after 10 minutes in boiling water in an insulated container). Celery, in particular, may take a while to return to the land of the edible, so it may require extra soaking time. Carrot flakes, shredded carrots, and carrots that have been sliced very thin will work in instant recipes.

If you are putting together the ingredients for an instant dish, do not use a vegetable mix that includes dehydrated peas or corn, or square chunks of carrots or potatoes, because these vegetables take 20 or more minutes of simmering to rehydrate. Dehydrated corn and peas can be used in the backcountry if they're presoaked. See Substitutions, page 46, for more information on using dried peas and corn.

Freeze-dried vegetables, including asparagus, broccoli, corn, green beans, peas, potatoes, and vegetable flakes are available through mail order, and many backpacking stores sell individual portions of corn and peas.

Corn, green beans, and peas rehydrate very well and with a little butter powder make up nicely as individual side dishes. The other freeze-dried vegetables vary—generally either texture or taste suffers. These vegetables are useful when combined with other ingredients in instant soups, stews, and one-pot dishes.

While dehydrated corn and peas are hard as rocks, freeze-dried corn and peas (and some of the other freeze-dried vegetables) crumble easily. Use them early in the trip or pack them carefully for the long haul.

Tomato powder and spinach powder can add flavor to one-pot meals and soups. Although these powders are usually only available by mail order, stores that carry fixings for homemade pasta may have them in stock for use as pasta ingredients—it's worth calling if there's such a store nearby.

EGGS AND DAIRY PRODUCTS

Eggs: It is possible to carry eggs in the shell on trail, but they must be handled as the fragile commodities they are. It's unwise to carry raw eggs that have been broken into a plastic container because they are susceptible to salmonella (see page 45). Cartons of "fat-free egg product," which contain egg whites and other ingredients but no egg yolks, are useful only for the first morning out because for longer term storage they must be refrigerated.

Pasteurized powdered eggs are light and easy to pack, and they work well in baking. Doctored up, they make tolerable scrambled eggs. Pasteurized powdered eggs are germ-free when you buy them, but they can easily be contaminated with salmonella. See page 45 for information about handling and storing powdered eggs.

Egg substitute or replacer contains leavening plus potato starch, tapioca flour, and carbohydrate gum. Directions call for using 1½ teaspoons plus 2 tablespoons water to replace one egg. Add one more tablespoon of water to adjust for recipes in this book. If cholesterol is a concern, this is a good substitute for eggs in baked goods.

Buttermilk powder used in combination with baking soda provides leavening and flavor. Use ¼ cup powder to make 1 cup buttermilk.

Cheese is available fresh and powdered. The real stuff is vastly superior when you are eating cheese and *something* (crackers, tortillas, et cetera), but cheese powder works well as an ingredient in egg dishes, soups, stews, and one-pot meals. Parmesan and Romano have been around as shake-ons for years, but recently both white cheddar and orange cheddar have become available in powdered form—the same powders that are used in macaroni and cheese box mixes. Blue cheese powder is also available; mixed with mayonnaise, it makes a peppy blue cheese dressing.

Blocks of hard cheeses like Parmesan are good choices for warm-weather outings because they will not weep as much oil as softer cheeses like cheddar. Although people think of pasta when they think of Parmesan, in fact thin-sliced parmesan is quite tasty with crackers or tortillas. Individually packaged servings of string cheese, which is actually part-skim mozzarella, last well.

Sour cream powder makes up rather nicely. Be wary of buying this powder from a bulk container at a health food store; you don't know how long the powder has been sitting around unrefrigerated. Sour cream powder that has gone bad is really bad, so buy fresh and store it in the refrigerator or freezer. You can substitute (real) cream cheese, though it is heavier because it has more moisture.

Butter-flavored sprinkles can be found in the spices section of the baking aisle in the supermarket. Altough this product is easily obtainable, I prefer the flavor of pure butter powder.

Butter powder, which is available by mail order, has a mild butter flavor that enhances chowder, vegetable side dishes, one-pot meals, and baked items. It cannot, however, be used for sautéing, and butter powder on bagels won't win any awards.

Powdered vegetable shortening doesn't really belong in the dairy section, but is included here because it's similar to butter powder. Powdered shortening can be used for frying (it turns to liquid oil as it heats up), baking, and boosting calories. Note that it is concentrated; if the recipe calls for 1 teaspoon of oil or shortening, use ½ teaspoon powder.

MEAT AND SEAFOOD

Canned chicken and turkey have long been used by backpackers to add heft and flavor to a one-pot meal.

Freeze-dried chicken and turkey rehydrate tolerably well with the addition of water, boiling or otherwise. A little can go a long way when used as an ingredient rather than as a main course.

Comparison shopping is in order when considering freeze-dried

Canned turkey, chicken, shrimp, and tuna can be used sparingly but effectively to add protein and flavor to dinners.

versus canned. A 1-ounce package of freeze-dried chicken makes ⅔ cup chicken; a 5-ounce can of chicken (meaning 5 ounces of chicken not including the can) holds ⅔ cup. Freeze-dried costs almost twice as much as canned. The decision, then, involves a trade off-between weight and cost—in other words between knees and wallet.

Dried chicken and turkey are not, to my knowledge, commercially available. If you want to make your own, see the hints in Chapter 2. Some people say that rehydrated chicken and turkey meat has great flavor and texture, while others say it tastes like cardboard. One's reaction doubtless depends on a combination of drying technique, hunger, and personal preference. You can also brown and dehydrate ground turkey.

Freeze-dried beef, when reconstituted, comes close to the real thing. Like freeze-dried chicken and turkey, it is exceedingly light and an excellent choice when weight is a major concern.

Dried beef—the kind used in creamed chipped beef—contains enough moisture that it must be refrigerated after the jar has been opened. You can easily dry it a little more to make a handy addition to one-pot meals.

Dried ground beef is not available commercially but you can make your own; see Chapter 2 for instructions. Dried ground beef can be used in instant meals, and it costs about one-fifth as much as freeze-dried beef. The dried version, however, does weigh more. One-half cup dried ground beef, made from 1 cup cooked ground beef, weighs just under 2.5 ounces. One-half cup freeze-dried, cubed beef, by comparison, weighs just 0.75 ounce, or one-third the weight of its dried counterpart.

Pepperoni gets greasy in the heat but is fine in moderate or cold weather. A small amount can make a big impact in a one-pot meal.

Bacon is a potent ingredient that adds a meaty taste even when used in small quantities. Crumbled bacon and low-fat bacon morsels come in glass jars which, once opened, should be stored in the refrigerator. I buy the low-fat option and then dry it a little more so that it's really dry. Because of bacon's high fat content, dry mixes containing it should be refrigerated or frozen until it's time to take them on trail.

Cooked bacon strips packaged in an oxygen-free pouch will keep well without refrigeration for several months. The product I found in the supermarket has 20 strips of bacon. Because the contents should be refrigerated after the package is opened, it makes sense to use all the bacon within a short period of time.

Imitation bacon-flavored morsels offer an alternative to real bacon. The brands that are low in fat don't require refrigeration once opened.

Foods like pepperoni, a fresh kiwi or orange, and marinated artichoke hearts serve as valuable "trade" items on trips. These are the items that you'd die for on the ninth or tenth day out in the backcountry when everyone's pantry is stocked with hopelessly uninteresting meals and the few select treats that looked so good in the grocery store seem boring and repetitious. Now's the time to pull out your trade items and see what you can get for them.

—Sanna McKim

Freeze-dried shrimp are wonderful, delightful, scrumptious—and very expensive. They rehydrate quickly in hot or cold water and have the taste and feel of fresh shrimp. If money was not a consideration, freeze-dried shrimp would be at the top of my shopping list.

Canned shrimp are heavier than freeze-dried but not nearly as expensive.

Dried shrimp, which are available at Asian food markets, are small whole shrimp, shell and all. Dried shrimp are used in Asian cooking to make a shrimpy broth, but they cannot be substituted for either the freeze-dried or canned varieties. I find the flavor to be a little off, and the shells make the shrimp very chewy indeed.

Freeze-dried tuna fish rehydrates well and tastes more or less like canned tuna. Be aware that a pungent fishy odor does emanate from the used plastic bag, even when it's placed inside another plastic bag. (The smell is one more reason to bear-bag your trash.)

Canned tuna is an easy if heavy trail standby. Though you can make perfectly good tuna salad with canned or freeze-dried tuna, mayo packets, and fresh or rehydrated vegetables, if you want a quick spread, you might consider canned tuna salad or dry tuna salad mix.

Dry tuna salad mix is available through mail order. Add water, let stand a few minutes, and you have a reasonable version of tuna salad.

▲ ▲ ▲

How to Save Money when Buying Ingredients

Buy what you will really use: If you buy more than you need and don't use the leftovers, then you are losing money rather than saving it. But if you are happy eating corn or peas with regularity, then it makes sense to buy corn or peas in bulk.

Comparison shop: Get catalogs from all the companies that have ingredients you might want and compare their prices with the cost of the same (or comparable) products from the supermarket or health food store. If you are really counting pennies, compute the cost per ounce (be sure to include the cost of shipping—see below) to determine who offers the best price.

Comparison shop, continued: Also check the prices of various quantities purchased from the same company . For example, if 1.5 ounces of freeze-dried peas cost $2.40 ($1.60 per ounce), 3 ounces, $4.20 ($1.40 per ounce), and 16 ounces,

$15.20 ($0.95 per ounce)—and you can use 16 ounces of freeze-dried peas—it's a deal.

Put together a backwoods food coop order: If mail-order ingredients are sold in amounts too great for your needs, invite several trail friends to join you in a group order.

Remember that time is money: Hunting down every last bargain will save money, but sometimes it makes sense to take advantage of someone else's work. Sure, you can buy grapes, cut them in half, and dry them, but raisins are not that expensive. If you want to dry something for a special treat, slice up a few kiwi fruits to add sparkle to your snack bag.

Check the fine print regarding shipping: It pays to understand how you'll be charged. Some mail-order companies charge a percentage of the invoice (I've seen as low as 2 percent and as high as 10 percent). Others charge in stepped increments (say, $6.00 for orders $25.00 and under, $11.00 for orders $25.01 to $50.00, and so on). With stepped increments, the nearer you come to the higher limit of merchandise value, the less you pay, proportionately, for shipping. Still other companies charge by weight. Because of economies of scale, heavy orders cost less per pound than light orders. If you are buying an ingredient that costs $3.00 and weighs 8 ounces and the shipping for an order weighing 4 to 20 ounces is $4.00, then shipping charges equal 133 percent of the value of the order. If, however, you are buying $50.00 worth of ingredients that together weigh 5 pounds and the shipping comes to $6.00, then shipping equals only 12 percent of the value of the order.

SOUP

Instant soups of all varieties—ranging from black bean soup to corn chowder—are available at the supermarket. These easy-to-use mixes generally come in a paper container; all you have to do is add boiling water. When preparing for a trip, ditch the container and transfer the contents to a small plastic bag. Because these soups usually contain freeze-dried beans, veggies, and other ingredients, they can be combined with a quick-cooking carbohydrate like bulgur or couscous to fill out a meal. However, because the soup is spiced for

The author's test kitchen.

one cup of food, if you add a carbohydrate, you'll need to add extra seasonings.

Dehydrated soups also come in many flavors and can be very handy when you want to add flavor and body to a dish. But let the user beware: Some dehydrated soups contain a whopping amount of salt—as high as two-thirds of the daily recommended amount. (For comparison, one cube of bouillon may contain 40 percent of a day's worth of salt, and low-salt alternatives ring in at 1 percent.) If you need to watch your salt intake be careful with dehydrated soups. Also, people with a sensitivity to monosodium glutamate (MSG) should probably avoid prepared soups. Several brands use MSG as an ingredient, and many others use ingredients such as autolyzed yeast and yeast extract that contain MSG.

Bouillon is available in supermarkets in both powder and cube forms and in regular and low-salt versions, though I've not found an MSG-free version. Because bouillon powder dissolves more quickly than a cube, I have called for powder in the recipes.

SAUCES

Gravy mixes are available at supermarkets. One packet generally makes one cup.

Cheese sauce mix is available from supermarkets. As an alternative, you can combine cheese powder and powdered milk.

Sweet and sour sauce mix purchased in the supermarket contains vinegar powder, an ingredient not available commercially. Because it is hard to have sweet and sour without the sour, and liquid vinegar is heavy, the dry mix has a place in the backcountry cuisine.

Dried pesto is available in packets in the supermarket and health food stores. Though not as tasty as fresh pesto, dried pesto is easier to carry.

CONDIMENTS

Ketchup, mustard, mayonnaise, relish, lemon juice, and other condiments are widely available in small packets at fast food restaurants and supermarkets. If you have extra left over from your order, save them; if not, negotiate with the management for a small supply. See page 45 regarding the use of mayonnaise on trail.

Salsa is available in small packets (see above)as well as in dehydrated form at some health food stores. It's also easy to dry salsa at home (see Chapter 2).

John Emelin's Hot Tips

John is proprietor of Uncle John's Foods, of Fairplay, Colorado, which makes air-dried vegetarian meals for outdoorspeople. He has also taught classes in outdoor cuisine.

Why plan: Three meals a day for each hiker, along with morning and afternoon snacks, don't fall into place without effort, and once you're away from your car, you can't correct the deficiencies. If you plan ahead, most of the work is done before you go, and you can enjoy the experience of being outside.

Measure in advance: Plan portions per person and actually measure them. Remember to plan and pack for variety. Don't fall prey to the attitude of "Well, *someone* will eat it." By the third day on the same dish, *no* one will eat it unless they have no other choice.

Emergency rations: Always allow one day's food per person extra for emergency rations. Each person should carry some food at all times.

Choosing ingredients: Don't make your trip an ordeal of preparation by insisting on preparing every last morsel yourself, especially if it's only going to save you a few dollars. If you didn't get the spaghetti sauce dehydrated last winter, and you don't have time to do it now, then find a substitute. Don't assume that you can do it more cheaply yourself. Remember that commercial producers often deal in such volume that they can make it and market it for less than you can make it at home, even if you count your labor as nothing.

Doctor the mundane: Look for dried meals at the supermarket, and use noodle, potato, and rice dishes for your base. Once you've perused the inexpensive dried meals at the supermarket, check specialty stores for extra ingredients to bring them to life. It only takes a few sun-dried tomatoes and a squirt of olive oil to turn noodles in cream sauce into something worth chewing. The key is variety. (For example, don't use the same mix of vegetables in every meal.) Consider losing the sauce mix provided with the packaged dinner and make your own. Use powdered milk; instant vegetable, beef, or chicken bouillon; cornstarch for a thickener; and tomato crystals or powder as the base for a soup or stew. Start with packaged gravy mix, use only part of the package (it usually contains too much salt), and stretch it with your own blend of powders.

Favorite foods: See John's Dessert to Die For (page 138) and Fruit Crisp (page 154).

Wasabi is a very strong horseradish powder. This slightly greenish condiment can be used to spice up almost any savory dish.

Salad sprinkles, which generally contain such ingredients as sunflower seeds, sesame seeds, some form of soy, and dehydrated vegetables, can be used to flavor eggs, cold lunch salads, and all manner of entrées.

SEASONINGS

All the recipes in this book include seasonings, but if you like to experiment, browse around in the seasoning packet section of your supermarket. There are lots of options—packets for stir fry dishes, lemon chicken, Mexican specialities, and so on—some of which are free of artificial colors or flavors.

Herb blends in the supermarket, health food store, or ethnic market also hold great possibilities. Herb blends allow you to experiment without buying the individual ingredients. Some blends, like curry, garam masala, and za'atar, are traditional, while others, like Mediterranean and Thai seasonings, have been created for the convenience of shoppers. All herbs, blends or not, should be stored in a cool, dry place to maintain freshness. (Above the stove is not a good storage area.)

Here are some common blends with their ingredients:

Chinese five-spice seasoning—or at least one version of this seasoning—contains anise, cinnamon, star anise, cloves, and ginger. Another brand contains fennel, anise, cinnamon, black pepper, and cloves. Use ¼ to ⅓ teaspoon per serving.

Creole seasoning may contain chili powder, salt, cumin, coriander, paprika, and cloves; other versions contain chili powder, garlic, parsley, salt, thyme, and cayenne pepper. Because brands may vary, test first, starting with about ½ to ¾ teaspoon for every ½ cup tomato sauce or ½ cup uncooked grain.

Curry powder in the supermarket represents only one of the many possible configurations of spices that form curry bases. Some curries are very hot, some quite mild; different types are used for different foods. Read the label closely to see what ingredients a particular brand includes. These three ingredient lists show the variety available: (1) turmeric, ginger, coriander, cardamom, cayenne pepper; (2) cumin, coriander, turmeric, fenugreek, black pepper, dried chilis, poppy seeds, cardamom seeds, cinnamon, mustard seed, ginger; (3) turmeric, coriander, cumin, dried ginger, peppercorns, dried hot peppers, fennel seed, mustard, poppy seeds, cloves, and mace. The amount to use depends on the proportion of other spicy ingredients and the age of the mix. Start with ¾ teaspoon per ½ cup uncooked grain and work upward to your level of comfort.

Herbs de Provence, a blend that takes its name from Provence, France, includes rosemary, marjoram, thyme, sage, anise seed, and savory. Use ¼ teaspoon per serving.

Ginger is a really versatile ingredient. Fresh ginger root is easy to carry, marvelously pungent, and stimulating, especially in winter. When you're really cold, a few slices boiled in water will perk you right up.

—Annie Getchell

Mediterranean seasoning may include salt, onion, spices (including chili pepper, oregano, fennel seed, cumin seed, red pepper, and garlic), red and green peppers, carrots, parsley, and turmeric. As with any seasoning mix, check for additives, such as autolyzed yeast extract, which often contains MSG. Use 1 to 1½ teaspoons of Mediterranean seasoning for every ½ cup uncooked grain.

Garam masala is a hot spice mixture from India that is made from black pepper, coriander, cumin, cloves, cardamom, and cinnamon. It is usually used with other seasonings, and the amount of garam masala depends on the amounts of those other seasonings.

Lemon pepper contains garlic, pepper, onion, citric acid, lemon crystals and oil, turmeric, and other spices and herbs; some brands are salt free. Use lemon pepper to taste.

Thai seasoning may include chili pepper, ginger, coriander, red pepper, cumin, cinnamon, star anise, salt, garlic, lemon peel, shallots, cornstarch, jalapeño peppers, and other flavors. Use ¼ to ½ teaspoon per serving.

Za'atar is a traditional Middle Eastern seasoning that includes thyme, oregano, roasted sesame seeds, salt, and sumac. Traditionally this spice is mixed into olive oil and spread on flatbread.

▲ ▲ ▲

Stocking Trail Ingredients

No, you don't have to run out and buy every ingredient listed in this book, but if there are ingredients that are new to you, and they look appealing, try them one by one to see if you want to include them in your repertoire. Once they are part of your larder, you can decide whether to keep supplies on hand or buy only enough for upcoming trips.

Your pantry will look different than mine, depending on what kind of cook you are, how often you head out to the backcountry, and how you travel when you get there. If you go out regularly, weekend after weekend, it makes sense to stock more ingredients than if you plan one big trip each year. Here is my way of organizing trail ingredients:

Ingredients I keep on hand because I use them in the home kitchen as well as on trips: Tomato flakes, green and/ or red bell pepper flakes, powdered milk, oatmeal, low-fat bacon morsels, salad sprinkles, wasabi, other condiments and seasonings

With a well-stocked cupboard of simple and varied ingredients, packing out trips can be relatively easy without short-changing the quality of your food.

Ingredients I keep on hand for at-home use but buy in quantity when preparing for a trip: Grains, pasta, Chinese noodles, dried fruit

Ingredients I keep on hand because the ingredients last and I know I'll use them up eventually: Dried mushrooms, freeze-dried corn and peas, cheese powder (stored in the refrigerator), butter powder (in the fridge), potato starch, orange powder, coconut cream powder

Ingredients that I buy or dehydrate myself, as needed for specific trips: Dried vegetables, some dried fruit, jerky

Ingredients that I buy from the supermarket when preparing for a trip: Instant hash browns, instant refried beans, black bean powder

Ingredients for which I plan ahead and buy from mail order companies as needed for specific trips: Freeze-dried meat, poultry, seafood, and vegetables

CHAPTER 2

Kitchencraft

The camp cook should take a pride in the artistic handling of his utensils, particularly in his ability to work quickly and to keep half a dozen things going at once; to keep the portions of the meal already cooked in a warm place; to keep the ashes out of the potatoes, and the ants from the sugar. Serve as near the fire as possible, and have hot water handy for washing dishes between courses.

A. D. Gillette and W. and S. McAndrew,
"Camp Cookery," *Outing* magazine, 1896

BACKCOUNTRY FAST FOOD AND LOW-FUEL COOKING

Surely one of the great advantages of freeze-dried food is that all you have to do is add boiling water and let the food stand 10 minutes. If you calculate how much gas you need to boil, say, a cup of water, then you can estimate the amount of gas you need for x number of dinners, breakfasts, and hot drinks, factoring in a multiplier—maybe 25 percent—for adverse weather conditions and a margin of safety. Your pack is lighter because you carry less gas, you have more free time to enjoy the sunset, and you never have to scour scorched-on mac and cheese from your pot.

But if you're on a tight budget or you'd rather design your own menu, you don't have to forgo the ease and speed of instant meals on trail—you can pack your own. The idea is to use ingredients that will rehydrate/cook in an insulated container (to maintain heat) in a reasonable amount of time (10 minutes). There are lots of ingredients that qualify, as you can see from browsing through the recipes marked with an asterisk (*) and reading the descriptions of ingredients in the previous chapter.

Fast-food recipes will not work as well, or they may not work at all, at altitude, where water boils at less than 212 degrees, or during the winter, when cold saps heat so quickly that the food does not cook fully. You can, however, use these recipes to decrease fuel use, for they will require much less simmering than recipes with longer-cooking ingredients.

One drawback to bulgur, couscous, and similar fine-grained foods which rehydrate quickly is that they lack texture because the individual bits of food are so small. Because texture is important in meal appeal, plan on serving something crunchy, such as bread sticks, crackers, toasted sunflower seeds, or nuts with these instant dishes.

▲ ▲ ▲

Adults Aren't the Only Ones Who Like Backcountry Fast Food

At the end of one trip I gave my friend Jean a bag of leftover Coconut-Mango Rice Pudding because she said Ian, her ten-year-old son, would be intrigued with the concept. She later wrote that Ian was "very impressed—both with the dessert and the minimal weight before hydration." He made the pudding himself and now wants to cook "that way" the next time the family goes out. He likes the idea that he can help prepare trip food by drying the tomatoes he gets from the garden and the wild blueberries he picks from a nearby field.

Jean observes that kids often feel left out of meal preparation on a trip—they (like their parents) may be tired at the end of a day and have little energy for fussing with dinner. They just need to eat, pronto. "What should be a time of thankful sharing sometimes turns into a time of burnt or sliced fingers, greasy hands and clothes, and short tempers!" Instant meals can help ease late-in-the-day meltdowns for young and old alike. The simplicity of prep and clean-up are also advantages when there are so many other pressing things to do.

Ilo Gassoway's Hot Tips

Ilo teaches a course in backpack cooking each summer for the Yosemite Association and has contributed articles and recipes to *BACK-PACKER* magazine. He has hiked through much of the western United States.

Style: I tend to be a one-pot gourmand. I want the food to be great tasting and I want there to be plenty of it. My two-person portions tend to feed four people. (See Ilo's recipes for Bagel and Fruity Cream Cheese, on page 50, Fruit Leather, on page 71, and Backpack Sukiyaki, on page 101.)

Favorite items: My cook kit includes a whisk, turner, spoon, grater, garlic, Tabasco, and bottles of seasoned rice wine vinegar, sesame oil, Kahlua and Rumplemintz. (The last two are great additions to chocolate pudding and/or hot chocolate.) In addition, I have a bag of seasonings I've collected from various fast-food locations—soy sauce, hot oil, hot mustard, BBQ sauce, ketchup, sesame seeds, salsa, and honey to name a few. I always have small plastic jars of cream cheese and peanut butter.

Gadget: If you are going to do much back-packing, then you should have a dehydrator. The cost is so small compared to all the money you save by making your own foods—not to mention the taste, which surpasses anything you can buy. Prepackaged food tends to be overseasoned to cover up the fact that the food itself has no taste. Dried foods have such a concentrated taste that once you've tried

them, you will never want to go back. And nearly everything can be dried. I've tried every-thing from marinara sauce to yogurt chews to tofu. The only thing I've been disappointed in were cucumbers (yuk!).

Food tips: For coffee, I use a small coffee ball (similar to a tea ball), put in a teaspoon of my favorite ground coffee, seal the ball, place it in my cup, and add boiling water. In a minute or two, I have a steaming cup of fresh coffee—and very little trash to carry out.

Trail wisdom: Recipes are made to be changed and adapted. Most of my recipes started out in one form and I changed them because of available supplies, weight consider-ations, or available cooking method—or simply because of the people on the trip and their taste buds.

Other suggestions: Try the recipes before you get out there and have no choice. Check out the portion size before you go, otherwise you will either waste food or starve. Adjust the seasonings to match your needs. Don't try to diet on a backpacking trip; you need calories to burn.

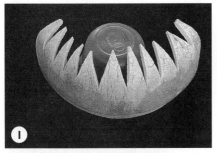

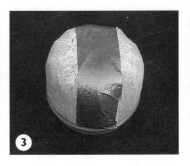

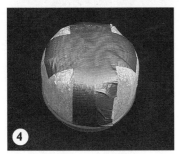

How to make a closed-cell foam cozy.

Insulating Your Containers

Having insulated containers is the key to boiling-water-only meals. The insulated travel mug with a lid is already a trail standby, so it doesn't need much explanation. Yes, travel mugs are bulky, but the advantage is that they can be purchased practically anywhere, and you don't have to do anything to adapt them for no-cook recipes.

Bowls can be bundled up in either a jacket made of closed-cell foam or a small cozy made from insulative fabric with a ripstop nylon layer to break the wind. The drawback to a closed-cell foam jacket is that it adds bulk to the bowl and may prevent efficient nesting; the advantage is that there is always an old closed-cell foam sleeping pad around, and you can make the jacket with a pair of scissors and duct tape. The cozy, on the other hand, takes up less room, but you have to locate material and know how to use a sewing machine. If you go the latter route, make the cozy fit loosely over the bowl so you can put it on and take it off with ease.

Although in ideal conditions a pot with a quart of water in it will retain more heat than a bowl containing two cups because of the increased mass, in less than ideal conditions some insulation is useful. You can be as casual about it as tossing a pile jacket over the pot once it has been removed from the stove (and you've made sure the pot isn't hot enough to melt the fabric), or you can use insulation specifically developed for the pot—either a cover you've made yourself, the aluminum tent used in convection-type bakers, or a heat exchanger. A homemade jacket of insulative material covered with ripstop nylon to block the wind can do extra duty as a pot bag. A drawstring or Velcro can be used to close the bag.

▲ ▲ ▲

Cozy Tests for Instant Meals

The hotter you can keep food, the better your instant meal will rehydrate and cook. No-cook recipes require a food temperature of at least 180 degrees Fahrenheit for 10 minutes.

The following test, which was done in a home kitchen, shows the temperature after 10 minutes for containers with various types of insulation. The tests did not simulate field conditions, which may include wind and cool evening temperatures.

Cup or mug filled to brim	Temperature after 10 minutes
Plastic cup without lid	150 degrees
Travel mug without lid	165 degrees
Travel mug with lid	180 degrees
Bowl with 2 cups boiling water	
Bowl with lid	175 degrees
Bowl with lid and homemade cozy	180 degrees
Bowl with lid and closed-cell foam jacket	180 degrees
Pot with 4 cups boiling water	
Pot with lid	180 degrees
Pot with lid and homemade cozy	190 degrees
Pot with lid and insulative jacket used in convection-type bakers	185 degrees

Saving Fuel

Instant meals are a major way to save fuel, but there are other things you can do that will make a difference:

- Make sure your stove is tuned up and ready to go so you don't waste gas trying to get it started.
- Before you light your stove, have a pot of water at hand so you can put it on immediately.
- Heat only the amount of water you need.
- Don't boil when simmer will do.
- Use a lid.
- Use pots that have been blackened (they will absorb the heat better).
- If they are compatible with your stove, use devices such as reflector collars and heat exchangers that conserve heat or fuel and block the wind.
- Use a windscreen if—and only if—your stove is designed to accommodate one. Some tank-underneath stoves will become overheated when a windscreen is used.

Regardless of how much fuel your system conserves, you still come down to the ultimate question: How much fuel should you carry? The best way to anticipate fuel needs is to keep notes on how much you used in past trips. Barring that, you can go by someone else's rule of thumb. In summer, for example, the National Outdoor Leadership School issues ⅙ quart (2.7 ounces) of fuel per one person per day on trail; in winter, the school allots ⅖ quart (6.4 ounces) per person per day. NOLS students cook with basic foods, however, not freeze-dried meals or instant meals.

DEHYDRATING FOOD AT HOME

Most of the recipes in this book call for ingredients that you can buy in their dehydrated form, such as dried tomatoes, onion, peppers, fruits, and so on. But sometimes it's easier to dry food at home than to scout around for ingredients and put them all together on trail. And with a little extra drying at home, you can take on trail products like bacon morsels and dried beef, which should normally be refrigerated. If you plan strategically, you can dry some very useful products with a minimum of effort.

Spaghetti sauce is a prime example. Sure, it's possible to combine tomato powder and various seasonings to make an acceptable backwoods spaghetti sauce. I did it for years. But if you want the taste of a long-simmered sauce in which the flavors have had time to develop and mature, buy spaghetti sauce from the supermarket and dry it at

©Jeff Scher

If your stove is compatible with a windscreen (top), reflector collar, and heat exchanger (bottom), use them to save fuel.

home. The process is not complicated—you don't even have to own a dehydrator.

Prepare the food you want to dry as described below, place it on a non-stick tray, and put the tray in the oven. The oven door must be open slightly in order for the moisture given off by the drying food to dissipate. The normal "door ajar" setting for broiling provides an opening of 3 to 4 inches, which is too much for my energy-miser standards. I put a wooden spoon across the corner of the oven door to crack it open about an inch.

Although people around the world have been dehydrating food for thousands of years without ovens or gauges, it is helpful to use an oven thermometer if you plan to do more than an occasional batch of spaghetti sauce. An inexpensive thermometer will set you back less than $5.00.

Drying time depends on the character of the food being dried, the thickness of the sauce or slices, and the humidity. Drying food at too high a temperature will result in case hardening—the outside will be hard but the inside will still be soft. Foods that are case hardened have not dried adequately and will not last well.

If dehydration appeals to you, then a dehydrator makes sense because it is energy efficient, has multiple trays so you can do more food at one time, and will dry items more quickly. Good dehydrators have a thermostat for temperature adjustment and a fan to circulate warm air so that food dries evenly. Special plastic screening for wet foods like tomatoes and plastic trays for liquids like tomato sauce are extremely useful. Dehydrators are available at outdoor stores, hardware stores, and appliance stores and can also be ordered through some mail-order outdoor and gardening catalogs.

Spaghetti sauce and salsa are my two top choices for home dehydration, but you can dehydrate individual ingredients (vegetables, fruits, and meats) as well. Here are some tips for home-drying:

Spaghetti sauce: If you have a favorite brand, buy a jar and dry the contents; you already know that you like it. Don't pick the cheapest sauce unless you are willing to live with the cheapest flavor. Sauces that include mushrooms, bell peppers, and other veggies as ingredients take longer to dehydrate because of the chunky individual bits of vegetable. You can either go with the longer drying time or buy a sauce without the chunks and add veggies later.

For oven drying, pour the sauce onto a non-stick cookie sheet, making a very thin layer. Place the pan in your oven and turn on the oven at the lowest possible setting, aiming for 130 degrees. For drying in a dehydrator, line the plastic tray with clear plastic wrap and spread

Because the "warm" setting on stoves is not exact, an oven thermometer is useful when drying food (top).

Commercial dehydrators should come with a built in thermostat (bottom).

sauce in a thin layer. (Sauce placed directly on the tray tends to stick.) Dry for several hours, or until done.

When testing the spaghetti sauce for doneness, remember that the dried sauce (leather) will be slightly more pliable when it is warm (just out of the oven or dehydrator) than when it cools. Remove the tray or a sample piece, let it cool a few minutes, and then test. Also, the leather comes off a cookie sheet more easily when it is pliable, so when it is almost but not quite done peel it off and reset it loosely; there is no need to do this when you are using a plastic-lined dehydrator tray.

If you are drying sauce with a specific recipe in mind, dry the amount you need. Otherwise, dry in one- or two-cup portions and clearly label the bagged results. (For example: "Add 1 cup water to make 1 cup spaghetti sauce.") Let the eater beware: Tomato sauce and salsa are indistinguishable when they are dry.

Salsa: See instructions for spaghetti sauce above.

Ground beef: Buy the leanest ground beef you can find, because fat shortens the shelf life of dehydrated foods. Brown the meat in a skillet, breaking it into very small pieces and making sure that there is no rare meat remaining. Put the beef on a non-stick tray and crumble any remaining chunks; the meat will dry, and later rehydrate, more quickly if all of the pieces are small and similar in size. Dehydrate at about 130 to 140 degrees until the pieces are dry and hard to the touch, about 2 to 4 hours. Drying time depends on the size of the pieces of meat and the temperature of the oven. One pound of ground beef yields about 3 cups cooked, which produces about 1½ cups dehydrated. Store in refrigerator or freezer.

If you are planning on using rehydrated ground beef with a specific recipe, you can add the seasonings called for in that recipe and allow the flavors to cook into the meat. Another option is to add a little flour to the beef as it cooks, so that when you use the meat in a recipe, water will not only rehydrate the beef but will also make up gravy.

Some books about dehydrating food describe a process for making beef jerky from raw ground beef. Because the temperature for drying is not high enough to kill bacteria—such as the virulent form of E. coli that has caused problems in undercooked hamburger—it is wise to forgo ground beef jerky and stick with ground beef that has been thoroughly cooked and dried. (Regular beef jerky is made of strips cut from a piece of raw meat and then dried. Bacteria cannot penetrate the surface of the meat, so there is less danger. It wouldn't hurt, as a precaution, to wash the piece of meat before slicing it. If the meat is partially frozen it is easier to cut into thin strips.)

Kristin Hostetter's Hot Tips

Kristin is *BACKPACKER*'s Equipment Editor. She recently took her mom backpacking for the first time, and confirmed that good eats help anyone make the transition from civilization to wilderness. Mom reports that the Backcountry Burritos (see page 122) were "awesome" and the cheddar and salami bagel was "the best sandwich" she ever had. But what amazed her most was how good the gorp tasted.

Style: I'm part pragmatist and part gourmand. When I'm alone, my cooking gear is minimal—one pot—and I eat soups, ramens, and samples of dehydrated stuff that various companies send us to test. When I'm with a group, however, I like to impress. Even if it's just one other person, I like to make dinners special (but breakfasts and lunches are basic). Not too fancy, but tasty. I do pizzas and focaccia, pastas with fresh and/or home-dried veggies, lentil chili, Backcountry Burritos (a guaranteed hit). There is always lots of fresh garlic—the ultimate backpacking food—in my dinners and fresh chopped jalapeños or other hot peppers if my compatriots like the heat.

Standbys: For breakfast, I serve good strong brewed coffee and oatmeal. In big groups I go with individual packets of instant oatmeal (two per person) with plenty of powdered milk and home-dried fruit (kiwis, nectarines, pears, apples, peaches, strawberries, cranberries, et cetera) on the side. Maybe a handful of gorp. The packets make life much easier because people can eat when they're ready, and there's no pot to clean up. With smaller groups of three or so, I usually make a pot of oatmeal and mix in cinnamon, nutmeg, coconut, and fruit.

Gadgets: On those big *BACKPACKER* test trips, I use a kitchen pouch that organizes all my spices in mini plastic bottles. I like my dehydrator but haven't used it to the max yet. The best thing I've dried in it is homemade hummus. I was skeptical about how it would rehydrate—it looked like kitty litter—but it came out wonderfully.

Trail wisdom: Having too much food is always better than too little. People get wickedly hungry in the outdoors and somehow a good meal always seems to disappear, even when you think you made way too much. Plus, if it was good for dinner, it'll be just as good for breakfast or lunch.

On a pack test in Oregon once I ran out of food on the last day. Before the grueling hike out I fortified my troops with a breakfast of shots of grape jelly, Dijon mustard, and Parmesan cheese. We boogied down that ten-mile trail and made a beeline for the nearest cowboy bar where (out of guilt) I treated everyone to burgers and fries.

Machaca: Machaca, a Mexican ingredient, is beef that has been simmered, flaked, and then dried in the sun. I have not made machaca, but John Emelin has, and he says it's great. You can improvise by using almost any type of meat—beef, ham, lamb, corned beef, chicken, or turkey, but not pork. John's directions go like this: Simmer the meat in water until it falls apart; cooking the meat helps break it into small pieces that will rehydrate easily later. Cool the meat. Remove as much as you can of the fat that has congealed on the surface of the broth and around the meat. Pull the meat apart and dry it in an oven or dehydrator. Store in a cool, dry place. (I recommend a refrigerator or freezer because there may be a little fat remaining, and keeping the food cold will retard the process by which fat goes bad.)

Dried beef: Dried chipped beef in gravy over toast may not be as popular as it used to be, but dried beef can be useful on trail. First, though, you need to dehydrate it completely so that when it is left unrefrigerated, it won't spoil. Spread the thin slices on a non-stick tray and proceed as for ground beef. Check every half hour, because the beef will dry quickly.

Ground turkey: You can dry ground turkey, but because it has lots more fat than lean ground beef, it will have a greasy feel. When cooked, ground turkey looks and tastes a lot like ground beef. Why bother with greasy turkey when you can get lean beef?

If you do choose to dry ground turkey, pour off the fat as the turkey is browning and spoon the browned turkey onto paper towels, which will absorb some of the fat. Then dry and store as you would ground beef.

Cooked turkey: See page 82 for a recipe for Spicy Teriyaki Turkey Jerky. **Never** dry uncooked poultry, which may contain salmonella (see Using eggs and mayonnaise on trail, page 45).

Bacon: Buy a jar of precooked and reduced-fat bacon (less fat equals longer storage), sprinkle the contents onto a non-stick tray, and dry the contents as you would ground beef. Store the dried bacon in the freezer and use it as you need it. Even though this bacon has less fat than strips of bacon from the frying pan, it should be used sooner rather than later.

Tofu: See page 101 for tips on drying tofu.

Fruits and vegetables: Because so many dried fruits and vegetables are now available commercially, only a quick overview is given here.

To dry fruits and vegetables, slice them about ⅛ inch thick. Some people prefer thicker slices, but these will take longer to dry. Vegetables except for carrots, tomatoes, bell peppers, and onions should be blanched (steamed or partly cooked). Fruit does not need to be blanched but may be dipped in lemon juice or a solution of ascorbic acid and water to prevent it from turning dark. Use good quality, unblemished fruit and vegetables and dry them when they are at the peak of ripeness.

Then, lay the pieces of fruit or vegetables on the tray. The pieces can touch but should not overlap. The ideal temperature is 135 degrees for drying fruit and 130 degrees for vegetables. As a rule of thumb, fruits should be leathery and veggies brittle.

Although I have dried all kinds of fruits and vegetables, my favorite is kiwi. Even a few slices, with their beautiful pattern of black seeds embedded in the bright green fruit, are a hit as a snack or dessert.

BAKING IN THE BACKCOUNTRY

A new crop of baking devices has changed trail food forever. Sure, you can stick with quick one-pot meals when you're making the miles, but for a slower-paced trip or a layover day, it sure is nice to cozy up to some cornbread or pizza. There are three types of backpacking bakers on the market, and there is a fourth way to bake that doesn't require a device.

The boil-in-a-bag type baker is the lightest of the devices. It consists of a one-inch aluminum grid surrounded by a two-inch collar that forms a heat exchanger. When placed in a pot with about an inch of water, the grid transfers heat from the pot to the batter, which sits atop the grid in an oven bag (check the plastic bag section of your supermarket). While this device won't produce a browned crust, it positively will not burn dinner or dessert, a plus for those who are easily distracted or have shaky culinary skills. Because the food is mixed and boiled in a plastic bag, there is no clean-up.

The Bakepacker™ is an example of a boil-in-a-bag type baker.

The Banks Fry-Bake Oven™ is an example of a backpacking Dutch oven (top).

The Outback Oven™ is an example of a portable convection oven (bottom).

Pack carefully so you take only what you need.

The backpacking Dutch oven includes an anodized aluminum frying pan with a sturdy surface and a tight-fitting lid with a shallow well to accommodate a twiggy fire. This device works like a regular Dutch oven but is much lighter and more compact. The pan can be used for frying, too. The key to using this oven is to keep the stove on low, so as not to burn what's in the pan, and maintain a twiggy fire on top. About one-third of the heat should come from below and two-thirds from above. The top heat produces a browned crust.

The lightweight, portable convection oven includes several parts. A heat reflector pushes the heat up and away from the stove base, a diffuser plate spreads the heat along the undersurface of the pot, and an aluminum-fiberglass tent placed over the pot forces the hot air up and around the pot so the baked goods are heated from all sides. A thermometer with settings of off, bake, and burn allows you to adjust the heat as needed. This device also produces a browned crust. The aluminum tent doubles as a heat conserver when cooking or when letting no-cook dishes rehydrate. The non-stick pan also doubles as a frying pan, though it requires gentle treatment because it scratches easily.

A small oven bag can be used to produce surprisingly good cakes and muffins for one or two people. Mix batter right in the bag, tie the bag closed, and then place it in boiling water for 10 minutes. The resulting cake or muffin isn't fancy, but it does taste good. As with the boil-in-a-bag type baker, there is no mess to clean up. (For more information on this system, see pages 62 and 141.)

LEAVE NO TRACE
OF YOUR BACKCOUNTRY KITCHEN

The backcountry is no longer wilderness. Chances are someone has been to your campsite before, and the less impact they've had, the more you'll enjoy your own stay. Here are some suggestions for keeping a Leave No Trace kitchen.

When you are packing food for the trip, try to gauge carefully how much food you will need so that there will be little, if any, food left over. If there are leftovers, save them for the next meal or pack them out with the garbage but never bury them.

Campsites should be at least 200 feet from rivers or lakes to minimize impact on those water bodies.

Because the kitchen is the social hub of a campsite, it gets the most traffic and is best sited on a durable surface to reduce impact on ground cover. Be careful to prevent small bits of food from falling on the ground as you cook and check the kitchen area carefully for debris when you are preparing to leave.

All of the recipes in this book can be made on a camp stove. The only time a fire is needed is as a twiggy fire when using a Dutch-oven type baker. Camp stoves eliminate all the problems associated with an open fire—disposal of partly burned wood and ashes, creation of a fire scar, destruction of habitat at a campsite in the quest for firewood, and the residue of unburnable detritus that lingers in a fire pit.

Sand and snow work well as pot and bowl cleaners; follow with a rinse of boiling water if the food was greasy or if you're with a group. If you must use soap, use only a little of the biodegradable variety. Strain wash water through a bit of screening or cheesecloth and pack out the dregs. Clean-up chores should be done on a durable surface at least 200 or 300 feet from a lake or stream. To spread out impact, choose an area somewhat separate from the kitchen site.

Scrubbing with snow is an easy (and soapless) way to clean pots in winter.

STAYING SAFE FROM CRITTERS LARGE AND SMALL

Gone are the days when you could assume that water in the backcountry is safe. With the spread of Giardia lamblia, cryptosporidium, and other organisms that can wreck your digestive system, it is imperative to purify the water you use on trail.

There are two dependable methods of purification: boiling and a combination of filtration and treatment with chemicals. Authorities differ on the amount of time water should be boiled; most say that bringing the water to a boil is adequate, though the Center for Disease Control recommends three minutes to ensure that viruses (like those that cause hepatitis) are dead.

The second alternative involves using both filtration and iodine. The problem with filtration alone is that it cannot remove viruses, while iodine alone, although it kills viruses, does not destroy cryptosporidium. A good water filter should combine both a filtration system to strain out bacteria and protozoans and an iodine chamber to kill viruses.

The other problem in the backcountry is with larger critters. When heading into bear country, check with park rangers and Forest Service personnel to see if there have been reports of bear–human encounters. It is imperative to keep your kitchen, food, and the smell of food well away from your tent site; 100 yards should be adequate. Also, keeping a clean kitchen—putting crumbs and cooking scraps into a plastic bag instead of letting them settle into the ground—will minimize smells.

Use a water filter with an iodine treatment chamber or boil to purify water.

Protect food from critters in summer and winter. This pine marten dragged off food that was stored on the porch of a cabin.

Place anything with an odor—food, garbage, toothpaste, sunscreen, the bandanna you used for a dish cloth and pot holder, even clothes permeated with the smell of food—in a bag and hang it from a tree limb or a line strung between trees or bear poles. The bag should be at least 8 feet off the ground and at least 4 feet from the tree trunk(s). Some parks, as an alternative, require the use of special bear-impervious lockers or portable plastic containers.

Mice, raccoons, and other animals can also cause food problems. The solution, again, is to keep food sequestered. For example, in a shelter or hut—where mice are often rampant—a tin can lid can foil mousy intruders. Make a hole in a tin can lid, then make a knot in the middle of a piece of cord, and slip the lid onto the cord. Tie the lid end to a nail in the shelter and tie the knot end to your food bag. The lid will prevent mice from running down the cord to your food bag.

▲ ▲ ▲

I always take a mesh bag with me for hanging food in bear country. The bag is light and easy to string up in a tree, and in the morning when all I want out of it is the coffee, I can see it through the mesh and don't have to dig, dig, dig. I pack everything in waterproof bags so that even though the mesh bag is not waterproof, things will stay dry.

Of course, I always check camp for a suitable bear-bagging tree and string the food line up before dark, even if it hangs for hours until I finish cooking. It can be difficult searching for just the right tree and stringing a bear bag in the dark.

—*Jeff Rennicke*

PART II

RECIPES FOR BACKCOUNTRY COOKING

Read This First

The next six pages present information that will help you make the best use of the recipes, including instructions for making substitutions and enlarging recipes.

ABOUT THE RECIPES

No-cook (instant) meals: Recipes that require only the addition of boiling water are marked with an asterisk (*). These recipes have been tested at sea level at an ambient temperature of about 70 degrees using an insulated mug or bowl. If you are camping at high altitude or in the winter, or if you don't use an insulated container, you may need to simmer no-cook meals for several minutes.

▲ ▲ ▲

Suit Yourself (and Your Friends)

With individually packed instant breakfasts, soups, beverages, dinners, and desserts, you and your partners can eat what you want, not what the other person decides to cook. You can have International Couscous while someone else has Unstuffed Potatoes and yet someone else has Tamale Pie Freestyle. All you need is a pot of boiling water.

Insulated bowl and cup: Instant meals require the use of an insulated bowl or cup. Insulated plastic travel mugs work well, and it is easy to make an insulated jacket for your bowl. Under ideal conditions, a pot that holds 4 or more cups of food will retain enough heat to make no-cook recipes, but you may want to insulate your pot, too. See Chapter 2 for insulation tips.

Ingredients: If you are reading a recipe and come across an ingredient you don't recognize, check the descriptions of ingredients in Chapter 1; then see Appendix A for information on where to find it.

Using fresh ingredients: Recipes in this book call for dried vegetables, but you can substitute fresh ones if you wish. Use the Substitutions and Equivalents chart on page 47.

A Packing Trick

When you have two ingredients you want to keep separate and you want to use just one bag, place one ingredient in the bag and tie off that section. Then place the other ingredient in the rest of the bag and tie or seal the bag. Place whichever ingredient you need to use first on top.

Storing food: All dehydrated food, including prepared trip meals containing dried food, should be stored in a cool, dry, dark place until you are ready to use it. Shelf life varies, but dehydrated fruit and veggies have the most flavor when used within a year. Any mixes containing dairy products (including powdered eggs) or fats (including nuts, seeds, and oil) should be stored in a refrigerator or freezer to prevent spoilage. Shelf life is less than a year.

Rehydrate first, then add salt: Dried food rehydrates more quickly without salt or salty seasonings. Many of the recipes are written so that the salty seasonings are added later.

Portions: Breakfast recipes generally make 1 to 1½ cups; dinner recipes 1½ to 2 cups; and dessert recipes, ½ to 1 cup. These one-person recipes are designed for one "medium" eater and serve as the baseline for making larger portions. It's easier to double a recipe than it is to cut it in half. If you prefer a larger portion, double the recipe. If there are two of you, double the recipe (or triple it or quadruple it, according to your eating needs). Use the Enlarging Recipes chart on page 48.

Nutritional information: Each recipe gives the number of calories and the grams of fat, carbohydrate, and protein per serving. Use these figures, along with the amount, as a guide when planning meals.

▲ ▲ ▲

How Many Calories Do You Need?

The number of calories you need per day depends on your metabolism and the activity at hand, but as a general guide a demanding day on trail can require twice as many calories (say, 3,800 calories for a 100-pound person and 5,600 calories for a 200-pound person) as would a sedentary day back home.

Recommendations for the source of those calories vary, but the bulk—50 to 60 percent—should come from carbohydrates. Complex carbohydrates (bread, grains, pasta, and other grain-based foods) should be the main source, with simple carbohydrates (fruit, sugar, honey) providing the balance. Proteins (meat, milk, and cheese as well as grains and beans to a lesser degree) are used to build tissue and should make up about 10 to 15 percent of the calories. Fats have more than twice as many calories per gram as carbohydrates and proteins, so they are an efficient way of carrying calories, but they should contribute only 20 to 25 percent (some authorities go as high as 30 percent for challenging outdoor activities).

Using eggs and mayonnaise on trail: Salmonella are bacteria that can wreak havoc with your gastrointestinal system. Because eggs are a terrific medium for growing salmonella, it's important to handle raw eggs and egg products carefully.

Do not carry raw eggs in any container except their own shells. Even breaking them into a clean container may expose them to bacteria.

Because mayonnaise contains raw egg, add mayo to a dish just before you eat it; don't save extra mayo or leftover food with mayo in it for later; and make sure that your bowl and spoon have been cleaned thoroughly. Small packets of mayo are ideal for use on trail.

Although pasteurized powdered eggs are germ-free when you buy them, they can easily be contaminated with salmonella that may be present on your hands or utensils. To minimize contamination, follow these guidelines: Make up a solution of soap, water, and a small amount of bleach. Wash your hands, the counter, and the spoon that will be used to scoop the eggs from their original container. When making a mix that requires powdered eggs, use a new rather than a recycled plastic bag. After you have opened a package of powdered eggs, store the package in the refrigerator. Likewise, store food bags with ingredients that include powdered eggs in the refrigerator. Also consider using an entire package (backpacking food companies make powdered eggs in convenient 2-person and 4-person quantities) at a meal rather than purchasing a half-pound or one-pound bag of dried eggs and splitting the contents into several meals.

If you are packing food for a food drop and are not certain under what conditions the food will be stored—unrefrigerated, in hot weather, for some length of time—consider using egg replacer rather than powdered eggs in recipes for baked goods.

Oven bags for baking: Be sure to use oven bags, which are designed for high heat, for all recipes that call for baking in a bag. *Do not* use everyday plastic bags, which may not be strong enough and which may allow the transfer of plastic molecules to the food inside. To be on the safe side, use water in which oven bags have been boiled for washing rather than cooking; never use water boiled in an aluminum boil-in-the-bag baker for cooking.

SUBSTITUTIONS AND EQUIVALENTS

When substituting fresh vegetables for dried, decrease the water in the recipe by approximately 1 to 1½ tablespoons for every tablespoon of dried vegetables. Because fresh vegetables will not "cook" when soaked in boiled water for 10 minutes, they should be packed separately, then sautéd briefly in oil or steamed before they are added to the other ingredients.

There is some loss of volume when meat, fruit, or vegetables are dehydrated and then rehydrated. For example, one medium carrot, which equals about 1 cup sliced, dehydrates into a scant ½ cup of dried, sliced carrots. But when that ½ cup is rehydrated, it will not measure up to a full cup.

When substituting canned meat for freeze-dried, decrease the water in the recipe by about 1 tablespoon for every tablespoon of freeze-dried meat.

Many of the recipes in this book call for freeze-dried corn or peas. You can substitute the home-dehydrated form, but it takes a little extra planning. When peas (or corn) are called for in a recipe, pack the vegetable separately. It takes about 1½ to 2 hours to rehydrate peas or corn when you add boiling water and let the vegetable stand. To avoid a long wait for dinner on trail, in the morning put twice as much water (use boiling water if you want to speed the process) as vegetable in a container with a secure lid and let rehydrate during the day as you hike. At dinnertime, pour off the water and add the vegetable to the other ingredients. (If you pour the soaking water in with the water you're heating for the dinner, you'll gain a little extra flavor for your broth.) Decrease the amount of water called for in the recipe by about half the amount of freeze-dried vegetable. Because this process is not an exact science, adjust liquid to taste.

SUBSTITUTIONS AND EQUIVALENTS

Vegetable	Approximate equivalent
Bell peppers, dried, 1 tablespoon	About ⅓ fresh pepper; about ¼ to ⅓ cup chopped
Carrots, dried, 1 tablespoon	⅛ medium carrot
Corn, freeze-dried, 1 tablespoon	1 tablespoon frozen corn; ½ tablespoon dried
Mushrooms, dried, 1 tablespoon	2 tablespoons sliced mushrooms; 2 medium sliced
Onions, dried, 1 tablespoon	⅕ medium onion; about 2 tablespoons chopped
Peas, freeze-dried, 1 tablespoon	1 tablespoon frozen peas; about ½ tablespoon dried
Tomato bits or flakes, 1 tablespoon	About 3 tablespoons fresh tomato

Other ingredients

Bouillon powder, 1 teaspoon	1 cube bouillon
Butter powder, 1 teaspoon	1 teaspoon margarine
Cheese powder, 1 tablespoon	2 slices (½ ounce) cheese
Eggs, powdered, 1½ tablespoon*	1 egg
Garlic powder, ⅛ teaspoon	1 small clove
Ginger powder, ½ teaspoon	1 teaspoon minced fresh
Meat, freeze-dried, ½ cup	½ cup canned meat
Shortening, powdered, 1 teaspoon	2 teaspoons shortening

*The recipes in this book call for 1½ tablespoons of powdered egg and 3 tablespoons of water to replace one egg. If your brand of powdered eggs calls for a different ratio (say, 2 tablespoons of powder), adjust the amount of powder but still use 3 tablespoons water.

Large travel mug, 2½ cups; regular travel mug, 1½ cups; large bowl, 3 cups; small bowl, 2 cups; small spoon (the coffee-stirring and dessert size), 1 teaspoon; Lexan spoon, 1 tablespoon; spice container lid, 1½ teaspoons. A strip of tape marked to show 1, 1½, and 2 cup-amounts can make measuring easier when using large containers.

ENLARGING RECIPES

Original amount	x 1½	x 2	x 3	x 4	x 5	x 6
pinch (less than $\frac{1}{32}$ t)	1½ pinches	2 pinches	3 pinches	⅛ t	more than ⅛ t	almost ¼ t
$\frac{1}{16}$ teaspoon	less than ⅛ t	⅛ t	more than ⅛ t	¼ t	more than ¼ t	less than ½ t
⅛ teaspoon	more than ⅛ t	¼ t	more than ¼ t	½ t	more than ½ t	¾ t
¼ teaspoon	⅜ t	½ t	¾ t	1 t	1¼ t	1½ t
½ teaspoon	¾ t	1 t	1½ t	2 t	2½ t	1 T
¾ teaspoon	1⅛ t	1½ t	2¼ t	1 T	1 T + ¾ t	1 T + 1½ t
1 teaspoon	1½ t	2 t	1 T	1 T + 1 t	1 T + 2 t	3 T
1½ teaspoons	2¼ t	1 T	1 T + 1½ t	2 T	2 T + 1½ t	3 T
2 teaspoons	1 T	1 T + 1 t	2 T	2 T + 2 t	3 T + 1 t	¼ c
1 tablespoon (3 teaspoons)	1 T + 1½ t	2 T	3 T	¼ c	about ⅓ c	¼ c + 2 T
1½ tablespoons	2¼ T	3 T	¼ c + ½ T	¼ c + 2 T	½ c - ½ T	½ c + 1 T
2 tablespoons	3 T	¼ c	¼ c + 2 T	½ c	½ c + 2 T	¾ c
3 tablespoons	¼ c + ½ T	¼ c + 2 T	½ c + 1 T	¾ c	1 c - 1 T	1 c + 2 T
¼ cup (4 tablespoons)	¼ c + 2 T	½ c	¾ cup	1 c	1¼ c	1½ c
⅓ cup (5⅓ tablespoons)	about ½ c	⅔ c	1 c	1⅓ c	1⅔ c	2 c
½ cup	¾ c	1 c	1½ c	2 c	2½ c	3 c
¾ cup	1 c + 2 T	1½ c	2¼ c	3 c	3¾ c	4½ c
1 cup	1½ c	2 c	3 c	4 c	5 c	6 c

CHAPTER 3

Breakfast

I remember that while we sat by the fire that evening George produced from somewhere in the recesses of his pockets a New York Central Railroad timetable on which was printed a buffet lunch menu, and handed it to us with the suggestion that we give our orders for breakfast. Hubbard examined it and quickly said, "Give me a glass of cream, some graham gems, marmalade, oatmeal and cream, a jelly omelette, a sirloin steak, lyonnaise potatoes, rolls, and a pot of hot chocolate. And you might bring me also," he added, "a plate of griddle cakes and maple syrup."

Every dish on that menu card from end to end we thoroughly discussed, our ultimate conclusion being that each of us would take a full portion of everything on the list and might repeat the order.

Dillon W. Wallace, *The Lure of the Labrador Wild*, 1905

Caffeine addicts will swear that coffee gives them life in the morning, but there is no denying that the rest of breakfast provides the calories needed to hit the trail. At home, many people eat the same breakfast, day after day, even if they have other choices, and I've found this to be true on trail as well. A rotation of several breakfasts (such as one cold cereal, two different instant hot cereals, and eggs with fried potatoes or refried beans), combined with an occasional breakfast of pancakes, seems to provide plenty of variety.

There's even a school of thought that says, "Why not eat dinner at breakfast?" On the last day of one trip, we had a just-add-boiling-water chili in the morning so we could start promptly and saved the prolonged project of making buckwheat pancakes for supper.

This chapter includes some new twists on traditional recipes—see Power Oatmeal and Phil's Pesto Omelette—as well as some unusual concoctions like Cindy's Hash Browns and Jello. (Cindy Ross swears it's a family favorite.) There are also recipes for the cooking impaired (add cold water) and for backcountry chefs (cinnamon rolls).

COLD BREAKFASTS • • • • • • • • • • • •

Want a quick getaway? Conserving fuel? Here are a few breakfasts that require no heat.

Ilo's Bagel and Fruity Cream Cheese

One of Ilo Gassoway's favorite ways to start the day is with raisin-cinnamon bagels or oatbran bagels, some cream cheese, and a bit of fruit leather. He reports that cream cheese comes packaged in individual foil packets that hold up fairly well on trail. (As an alternative to the bagel, he says, warm up a couple of flour or corn tortillas, which pack easily and hold lots of topping.)

Ilo's other method of preparing for his breakfast bagel is to mix cream cheese and dried fruit at home and package it in a refillable plastic tube, the kind that is available in outdoor equipment stores. This method has the advantage of cutting down on trash created by individual-portion packaging.

At home, combine and blend well in blender:
**¼ cup dried strawberries or
raspberries
1 cup cream cheese**

Pack in refillable plastic tubes.

On trail, spread Fruity Cream Cheese onto split bagel for breakfast, or use it as a snack while you're on trail.

Servings: The cream cheese and fruit mixture makes ten servings of 2 tablespoons each.
Nutritional information: For 1 bagel and 2 tablespoons cream cheese mix, 326 calories, 10 grams fat, 49 grams carbohydrate, and 10 grams protein.

▲ ▲ ▲

How to Cut a Bagel Without Cutting Yourself

Hold bagel against a flat surface with the bagel between your thumb and first two fingers. Using a sharp knife, insert the blade below the point at which you are holding the bagel and make a downward cut. Rotate the bagel, repositioning your hand and the blade but always keeping the blade beneath your hand. Cut and reposition until the bagel is sliced in two.

You are more likely to cut yourself with a dull knife than a sharp one because cutting with a dull knife is more difficult and you need to use more force.

These directions may seem to be common sense, but as bagels have become standard household foods, the number of bagel-related injuries showing up in emergency rooms across the country has skyrocketed. (We can only guess about bagel-related injuries in the backcountry!) Don't become a statistic.

Bagel with Nut Butter

A backcountry trip is a great excuse to treat yourself to luscious nut butters. Look for them in your health food store if they are not available in your local supermarket. I can never decide which I like better—almond butter, cashew butter, or walnut butter. Yum!

Nutritional information: For 1 bagel and 2 tablespoons almond butter, 341 calories, 12 grams fat, 49 grams carbohydrate, and 10 grams protein.

■

At home, place in a plastic bag and tie off:

2 tablespoons toasted chopped walnuts

In the rest of the bag, combine:

¼ cup plus 2 tablespoons bulgur

3 tablespoons dehydrated cranberries

1½ tablespoons orange powder

■

At home, combine in a large, flat pan:

10 cups quick oats
1 cup chopped or sliced nuts
½ cup honey
½ cup oil

Stir well and bake at 350 degrees for 30 minutes or until golden, stirring well after the first 15 minutes. Remove from the oven and add:

1 cup raisins and/or other chopped dried fruit
¾ cup wheat germ

Pack in one-portion amounts, adding:

⅓ cup powdered milk per 1 cup granoatmeal
or
½ cup powdered milk per 1½ cups granoatmeal

Cranberry-Orange Wheat Cereal*

This cereal is a not-too-sweet change of pace in the morning that requires no fuel at all. If you don't have orange powder, which I prefer, use orange-flavored breakfast drink.

On trail, add to the bulgur mixture:
    ¾ cup cold water

and let cereal stand overnight (a bowl with a lid comes in handy with this recipe). The bulgur and cranberries will rehydrate, and your cereal will be ready to eat in the morning. Add the walnuts and chow down.

Servings: Makes one serving of about 1½ cups.
Nutritional information: 459 calories, 9 grams fat, 89 grams carbohydrate, and 9 grams protein.

Granoatmeal*

This breakfast, which can be served with cold water as a fine-grained granola or with boiling water as oatmeal, gives you the flexibility to respond to the weather of the day.

On trail, add:
    1 to 1½ cups (or amount to achieve desired consistency) hot or cold water

Servings: The basic recipe (not including powdered milk) makes 12 cups.
Nutritional information: Per 1 cup granoatmeal plus ⅓ cup powdered milk, 558 calories, 28 grams fat, 62 grams carbohydrate, and 21 grams protein. Per 1½ cups granoatmeal plus ½ cup powdered milk, 837 calories, 42 grams fat, 93 grams carbohydrate, and 32 grams protein.

HOT CEREALS AND OTHER MORNING ENTICEMENTS • • • • •

Hot cereals don't have to take a lot longer to make. Boil a pot of water—half for your coffee, half for your cereal—and savor the java (and maybe a bagel) while the cereal is "cooking."

Instant Oatmeal*

Oats, which are a complex carbohydrate, and sugar, which is a simple carbohydrate, give you fairly quick energy, but by themselves they don't have much staying power—which is why you're hungry in a few hours when you breakfast on a bowl of oatmeal. When you eat a food with fat in it, you feel satisfied for longer because it takes time for the fats to be broken down and burned, and they therefore kick in after carbos are metabolized. To bolster oatmeal add ingredients such as: 1 tablespoon each coconut cream powder and shredded coconut (128 calories); 2 teaspoons margarine (67 calories); 2 tablespoons almond paste (133 calories); 2 tablespoons slivered almonds (64 calories); 1 tablespoon low-fat bacon morsels with 2 teaspoons butter powder (62 calories); 2 tablespoons chopped nuts (99 calories). Vanilla powder offers few calories, but it does provide wonderful flavor. And don't forget the powdered milk, which contributes needed protein.

Increase this recipe as your appetite dictates.

On trail, put cereal mix in an insulated cup or bowl and add:

1 cup boiling water

If you have added dried fruit to the cereal, increase the water by half the amount of the fruit. Stir well, cover, and let stand 10 minutes. Add more hot water if the oatmeal is too thick.

Servings: The oats, milk, and sugar in this recipe produce 1 cup of oatmeal. Add-ins will increase this amount.

Nutritional information: For basic oatmeal, 270 calories, 3 grams fat, 50 grams carbohydrate, and 13 grams protein. Additional ingredients boost the count.

How to make your own instant oats

If you like instant oatmeal but don't care for all the sugar that's in most supermarket brands, you can easily make your own by running quick (one-minute) rolled oats through a food processor until they reach a consistency similar to that of the oatmeal in the instant packet.

■

At home, pack together:
⅓ cup powdered milk
½ cup instant oatmeal
1 tablespoon (or to taste) sugar
pinch of salt (optional)
fruit, nuts, et cetera

Power Oatmeal Supplement

If you find the store-bought packets of instant oatmeal irresistibly convenient but want to increase the nutrients, make this power-packed supplement. Apricots provide vitamin A and wheat germ adds thiamin (B-1), niacin, vitamin E, potassium, phosphorus, zinc, and manganese. Dates pack a lot of carbos in a small space. Almonds and coconut cream powder together kick in fats. (If you don't have coconut cream powder in your larder, increase the almonds to 1½ tablespoons.) Because packets of instant oatmeal do not include milk, add powdered milk, which provides protein. This recipe makes 2⅓ cups power mix, enough for four servings of oatmeal.

At home, combine in a food processor:
24 small dried apricots, quartered
16 dates, quartered
1 cup wheat germ
½ cup sliced almonds
2 tablespoons and 2 teaspoons coconut cream powder
1⅓ cups powdered milk

Blend until ingredients are finely chopped. Store in a closed container in the refrigerator.

On trail, combine:
2 packets commercial instant oatmeal
½ cup plus 1 slightly heaping tablespoon power mix
1¼ cups boiling water (more to taste)

Servings: Makes one serving of about 1¾ cups.
Nutritional information: 729 calories, 19 grams fat, 133 grams carbohydrate, and 31 grams protein.

At home, combine:
¼ cup plus 2 tablespoons creamed rice
½ cup instant powdered milk
4 to 5 small apricots, sliced
¼ cup plus ½ tablespoon pecans, ground in blender

Apricot-Pecan Cream Cereal*

This cereal is a welcome change when you're suffering from oatmeal burnout.

On trail, put into insulated bowl and add:
1½ cups boiling water
Stir, cover, and let stand for 3 minutes. Stir again, cover, and let stand for 7 minutes more.

If you are using this recipe with a group, boil the water, add the ingredients, and stir well. Bring back to a boil and simmer for 30 seconds, continuing to stir all the while. Remove from heat, cover, and let stand 1 minute. Stir well and serve.

Servings: One serving of a little more than 1½ cups.
Nutritional information: 405 calories, 14 grams fat, 32 grams carbohydrate, and 9 grams protein.

Cheese Grits*

If you prefer to carry cheddar cheese powder (lighter, easier to handle, but not quite as tasty as the real thing if the truth be known) include 2 tablespoons with the grits and garlic.

On trail, dice cheese and place all ingredients in a bowl, and add:
   1 cup boiling water
Stir well, cover, and let stand a few minutes. Add salt and pepper to taste.

Servings: Makes one serving of 1⅓ cups.
Nutritional information: 270 calories, 4 grams fat, 44 grams carbohydrate, and 8 grams protein.

■

At home, combine:
¾ cup (two 1-ounce packets)
   instant grits
pinch garlic powder

Also pack:
1 ounce (one 1-inch cube)
   cheddar cheese

Grits with Butter and Maple Syrup*

Real maple syrup (available in granule form that doesn't leak) is good on anything. Yes, you can substitute brown sugar, but it just isn't the same. If you're going with the liquid stuff, put it in a small plastic container with a very secure lid.

On trail, place ingredients in a bowl and add:
   1 cup boiling water
Stir well and let stand a few minutes.

Servings: Makes one serving of 1⅓ cups.
Nutritional information: 377 calories, 3 grams fat, 80 grams carbohydrate, and 4 grams protein.

■

At home, combine:
¾ cup (two 1-ounce servings)
   instant grits
2 teaspoons butter powder
1 tablespoon plus 1 teaspoon
   powdered milk
2½ tablespoons (or more to
   taste) maple syrup granules

FROM THE FRYING PAN • • • • • • •

Why do fried foods taste so good on trail or off? It's probably the fat, which makes human taste buds sing. At least on trail, I burn off all those calories, so I never feel guilty chowing down.

Hash Browns and Scrambled Eggs

If ketchup is near and dear to your taste buds, pack a couple of individual-portion packets. Cheese powder, Tabasco, and/or rehydrated veggies like tomato bits, bell pepper, mushrooms, and hot pepper spice up eggs nicely.

For a Breakfast Burrito, warm up 3 (7½ inch) tortillas, wrap up the mixed eggs and hash browns, and lay on the salsa. If you like bacon, add some bacon morsels.

At home, place in the corner of a plastic bag and tie off:
4½ tablespoons (equal to 3 eggs) powdered eggs

In the rest of the bag, pack:
1 cup instant hash browns
1 tablespoon dehydrated onion (optional)

Also carry:
1 tablespoon oil

On trail, place instant hash browns in a pot or bowl, cover with boiling water, and let stand 5 to 8 minutes. Drain the water. Reconstitute the eggs according to package directions; you can use the leftover potato water when it has cooled to lukewarm.

Heat the oil in a frying pan and add the potatoes. Cook without stirring for 3 to 7 minutes until they are brown and crispy; use a pancake turner to turn them over and fry on the other side for about a minute. Push the potatoes to the side of the pan and cook the eggs until they are done to your liking. *Hint:* Because rehydrated eggs tend to be a bit rubbery, mix them right in with the potatoes to cook. That way, you get the egg flavor but the egg texture is broken up by the home fries.

If you are using a non-stick pan, you can make the hash browns this way: Mix instant hash browns, 1⅔ cups water, and oil in pan. Bring the water to a boil without covering, stirring a few times to keep the potatoes from sticking. Then simmer but do not stir for 3 to 5 minutes or until the water has been absorbed and the hash browns have browned. Turn the hash browns over and cook another minute or until the second side is brown. Add eggs as above.

Servings: One serving of 1¼ to 1⅓ cups.
Nutritional information: 582 calories, 26 grams fat, 63 grams carbohydrate, and 21 grams protein.

Potato Pancakes

Latkes, or pancakes made of grated potatoes, are a Jewish dish served at Hanukkah. Although potato pancakes are generally associated with dinner, they provide variety for breakfast. There are several acceptable box mixes on the market (after all, there aren't too many ingredients in potato pancakes), but if you'd like to make your own, here's the recipe. The powdered eggs and potato starch are both essential ingredients—they help the pancakes hold together and contribute to their capacity to brown. Traditionally, potato pancakes are served with applesauce (see recipe on page 155) or sour cream, but they are also good with eggs and a bagel.

On trail, add:

   1 cup cold water

and mix well. Let stand 3 to 4 minutes, then stir again. Spoon one fourth of the batter onto a lightly greased pan, forming a pancake a little less than ½ inch thick. Brown on both sides. Repeat with the rest of the batter.

Servings: Makes one serving of 4 pancakes, each of which is about 3½ inches in diameter.
Nutritional information: 225 calories, 4 grams fat, 39 grams carbohydrate, and 9 grams protein.

At home, mix well and pack together:
⅔ cup instant mashed potatoes
½ teaspoon salt
½ teaspoon powdered onion
2 teaspoons potato starch
1½ tablespoons powdered eggs (equal to 1 egg)

Tom Shealey's Hot Tips

Tom, who is *BACKPACKER*'s senior managing editor, grew up hiking the trails of the Great Smoky Mountains and paddling its rivers and lakes.

Style: I'm the biggest camp mooch there is. I always make sure I go out with someone who's a good cook. If that's not possible, then I stick to my tried-and-true menu: bagels, Snickers, and Kraft instant macaroni and cheese.

Trail wisdom: My biggest disaster was the time I made the mistake of hiking with a guy who's sole foodstuff consisted of cans of sardines. We shared a tent in a multi-day downpour in the Smokies. It smelled like rotten fish in there. To this day I can't eat sardines, even on a pizza.

The moral: What you take out there and eat is important, yes, but so is what your partner takes! In this case, it was merely olfactory displeasure, but I've been out with folks who were poorly prepared and sharing was in order. That made for a less-than-happy overall group because food supplies dwindled fast. Read: hungry campers. Before leaving, I always make sure I ask my fellow trail animals what they're planning to bring . . . so I'll know they're taken care of, and so I'll know what I can mooch!

▲ ▲ ▲

Cindy's Hash Browns with Jello "This probably sounds ridiculous but what we like to eat along side of hash browns is Jello. The sweet, fruity taste complements the potatoes and it resembles the jelly on toast that goes so well with fried potatoes. I never eat or make Jello at home but it tastes great with potatoes out there," says Cindy Ross.

You can use either dried potatoes from the store or those you make yourself. Cindy's advice for home-dried: Shred the potatoes, blanch them until they are somewhat clear, rinse off the starch, spread the shredded potato evenly in a thin layer on a dehydrator tray or a large oven tray. Sprinkle them with salt, pepper, and powdered onion, then dry them. (For more information on dehydration, see Chapter 2.) "They taste a little like potato sticks and my kids and I often eat half the bag before we cook them."

Soak the dehydrated potatoes the night before (which makes them even softer) or that morning and fry in margarine. If you decide to have Jello as a side dish, make it the night before when you are heating water for evening drinks. Add boiling water and then cold water per package directions, then let stand. Jello will set up overnight without refrigeration.

At home, combine:
1 cup instant hash browns
⅓ cup dried ground beef
2 tablespoons dried onion
1 tablespoon dried bell
    pepper (optional)

Pack separately:
1 tablespoon instant gravy
    mix

Carry in a secure container:
1 or more tablespoons oil

Beef Hash

Hash is good with eggs or by itself. Carry along some packets of ketchup or salsa to round out the meal.

On trail, place dry mix in a pot or bowl, cover generously with boiling water, and let stand for 10 minutes. If mixture absorbs all the water, add more. When potatoes and meat are rehydrated, drain off all but about ¼ cup water. Add the instant gravy mix, stirring well. Heat oil in pan and add hash, frying on one side and then the other. Season with salt and pepper to taste.

Servings: Makes one serving of about 2 cups.
Nutritional information: 489 calories, 18 grams fat, 71 grams carbohydrate, and 12 grams protein.

Phil's Pesto Omelet

When two of my friends went to their local L. L. Bean store to buy equipment, Phil Somers wound up putting their packs on a diet by showing them how to trim many pounds from what they had been carrying. Phil has gained his knowledge and acumen via twenty-five years of backpacking and snow camping, including winter peak ascents.

Phil considers himself a pragmatist when it comes to trail food. His breakfast standby includes eggs with veggies, pesto, and hash browns. He uses Eggbeaters on the first morning or freeze-dried eggs later in the trip.

On trail, chop and sauté onion and green pepper. Make the pesto sauce using 1 tablespoon oil and water per package instructions. Cook the eggs, then mix in the veggies and pesto sauce. Fry the hash browns, then place eggs on top of the potatoes and dig in.

Servings: Makes one serving of about 3 cups.
Nutritional information: 1177 calories, 48 grams fat, 145 grams carbohydrate, and 39 grams protein.

Phil's camp kitchen tip:

Use rubber gloves for clean-up, especially at colder times of the year.

At home, pack:
1 carton Eggbeaters (or other fat-free egg product equal to 4 eggs) or a 2½-ounce package of freeze-dried eggs
2 teaspoons pesto mix (from a store-bought envelope)
½ fresh green pepper
½ fresh onion
1 box (6 ounces) instant hash browns

Also carry along:
2 tablespoons oil

Fried Bread with Cinnamon and Sugar

Cindy Ross contributed this quick, easy, and very tasty addition to a leisurely breakfast (or leisurely dessert). Use Italian bread or a crusty round loaf that holds up well in your pack. Slice the bread, butter both sides, sprinkle a brown sugar and cinnamon mix on one side, and fry lightly over a low flame. Do the same with the other side. "It tastes a little like a sticky bun or cinnamon roll," says Cindy.

Nutritional information: Using 2 teaspoons butter or margarine and 2 teaspoons sugar mix with 1 slice bread, 162 calories, 11 grams fat, 22 grams carbohydrate, and 1 gram protein.

Michele Morris' Hot Tips

Michele is a senior editor at *BACKPACKER* who aims for a new outdoor challenge every year, the latest of which is whitewater kayaking.

Style: I would classify myself as a harried epicure—somewhere between a pragmatist and a gourmand. I look forward to good food (and plenty of it) when backpacking, and enjoy the preparation rituals both before and during a trip, but rarely have time to devote to creating new dishes or elaborate preparation. So, I compromise with good, tried-and-true recipes from reliable sources. I'll wing it on things like dried tomato sauce with added veggies (carrots, fancy mushrooms, sun-dried tomatoes, and textured vegetable chunks are my favorites) or random variations on oatmeal, and I'll occasionally splurge with biscuits, buns, or brownies.

Standbys: Cheese biscuits (a bagged instant buttermilk mix from the local Mennonite bulk food store with sharp cheddar and maybe some hot peppers) made with a BakePacker and refrigerated cinnamon buns that come in a cardboard cylinder are my favorites for lazy mornings, but only when I have willing help packing that heavy stuff in. (See Michele's Cheddar Buttermilk Biscuits on page 62.) If I'm making the gorp, I'll go for mixed fancy nuts, real chocolate bits, dried cranberries, dried peaches, et cetera.

Trail wisdom: Really good food can make up for a whole lot of blisters, mosquitoes, numb fingers and toes, and other minor backpacking annoyances. It's especially key for convincing skeptical first-timers.

BAKES ••••••••••••••••••••••••••

I've never been quite as adventurous with dough as Claudia Pearson, who reports on her version of breakfast nirvana: "Here's an idea that I discovered from a friend this summer. I make my bread dough the evening before, then stick the dough into a plastic bag and sleep with it in my sleeping bag. The next morning I punch it down, create something special, and bake it first thing. It's ready by your second cup of coffee! Nothing better than a hot cinnamon roll, a great view, and a steaming mug of coffee to start your day."

Here are several recipes for bakes that are somewhat easier to manage. For bready bakes, I generally use a ratio of two-thirds un-bleached all-purpose flour and one-third whole wheat flour, but for sweet bakes, I use all unbleached, all-purpose flour.

Irish Soda Bread

A plan-ahead cook might make this soda bread the night before, but chances are it wouldn't last till the morning. The combination of bak-ing soda and buttermilk helps leaven the bread and the buttermilk gives it a rich flavor.

On trail, add:
    ⅓ cup plus 1 tablespoon water
Mix well, either in the bag or in a pot. See page 62 for baking instruc-tions.

Servings: Full recipe makes 4 wedges.
Nutritional information: 217 calories, 7 grams fat, 33 grams carbohy-drate, and 4 grams protein per wedge.

Variation: Shortcut Irish Bread

If you don't want to bother with the buttermilk (delicious though it is), use 1 cup store-bought biscuit mix, 1 tablespoon margarine, and the sugar, raisins, and caraway seeds called for in the previous recipe. Bake as above.

Servings: Makes 4 large wedges.
Nutritional information: 200 calories, 13 grams fat, 20 grams carbo-hydrate, and 4 grams protein per wedge.

■

At home, combine:
1 cup flour
¾ teaspoon baking powder
¼ teaspoon baking soda
2½ tablespoons buttermilk
    powder
¼ teaspoon salt
1½ teaspoons sugar
2 tablespoons margarine or
    shortening

Stir well and then add:
1 teaspoon caraway seeds
¼ cup raisins

Michele's Cheddar Buttermilk Biscuits

Michele Morris added cheddar cheese to buttermilk biscuit mix on a trip to Denali and liked the results so much that it's now one of her favorite recipes. Michele uses a prepared mix, but you can easily make your own. Or, check your local supermarket to see if you can find something comparable. (For a shortcut, substitute ¾ cup plus 2 tablespoons of commercial biscuit mix for the flour, salt, and baking powder called for in the recipe.)

At home, combine:
¾ cup plus 2 tablespoons flour
¼ teaspoon salt
1 teaspoon baking powder
¼ teaspoon baking soda
3 tablespoons buttermilk powder
½ teaspoon sugar
2 tablespoons margarine
¼ cup powdered milk

Pack separately:
1½ ounces (1 by 1 by 1½ inch cube) cheddar cheese

On trail, cut cheese into small pieces, add to the dry ingredients, and mix well. Then add:
¼ cup plus 2 tablespoons of water
Mix well. See below for baking instructions.

Servings: Full recipe makes 4 wedges.
Nutritional information: 215 calories, 9 grams fat, 24 grams carbohydrate, and 7 grams protein per wedge.

■ ■ ■

Baking Instructions for Irish Soda Bread and Michele's Cheddar Buttermilk Biscuits

For a **backpacking Dutch oven (7 inches in diameter)** bake in a greased pan 15 minutes or until done. For a shorter baking time, use ½ the recipe, spreading very thin; bake 7 minutes.

For a **small boil-in-a-bag type baker (5½ inches in diameter),** using half the recipe with only 3 tablespoons water, boil/bake in an oven bag 12 to 13 minutes and let stand 3 minutes.

For a **large boil-in-a-bag type baker (7½ inches in diameter),** boil/bake in an oven bag 18 to 20 minutes and let stand 5 minutes.

For a **convection-oven type baker,** if your pot is 7 or 7½ inches, bring thermometer into the bake zone and bake 15 minutes. If your pot is smaller, bake a minute or two longer; if your pot is larger, bake a minute or two less. Use a greased or nonstick pot.

To make this recipe **with a frying pan,** use half the recipe with 3 tablespoons water and spread batter in a thin layer onto a greased pan; batter will look like a thick pancake. Cook over medium-low heat, covered, for 3 to 4 minutes, being careful not to burn the bread; flip the "loaf" over and bake another 3 minutes or until done.

To make these recipes **without a baking device,** use half the recipe, placing the ingredients in a small oven bag. On trail, add 3 tablespoons water and mix well. Close the bag with the tie that comes with it. Place in boiling water for 10 minutes and let stand 3 minutes.

Claudia Pearson's Hot Tips

Claudia has been rations manager for the National Outdoor Leadership School's Rocky Mountain Branch for twenty years and is coauthor of *The NOLS Cookery*.

Backcountry trends: (1) People can dry their own fruits, vegetables, and meats to take on trips. Food dehydrators, which are available at most hardware stores, can substantially reduce the cost of these items. For serious backpackers, a dehydrator is a worthy investment. If you go shopping for dried versions of the above you will often pay up to $8 per pound. If you buy these items in season and dry them on your own it can save you a substantial amount of money.

(2) Campfires are no longer allowed in many backcountry areas and that affects the elaborate campfire baking that backpackers have historically enjoyed. Sitting around the campfire telling stories and roasting marshmallows is quickly becoming a thing of the past! At NOLS we do most of our cooking over stoves with twiggy fires on lids as a top heat source.

(3) Meals need to be fast and easy to prepare but most importantly, there must be lots of food and it must taste good.

Biggest challenge: My biggest challenge is pleasing everyone. I issue a huge variety of foods in an attempt to please even the pickiest eaters. The diversity of tastes out there is amazing. Another challenge is getting people into the habit of eating and drinking frequently throughout the day so that they don't arrive at camp hungry, grouchy, and tired.

Texture is as important as calories, weight, and expense. In lunches, I include crunchy foods like animal crackers as well as a trail mix of pretzels, melba toast, those little fish crackers, and other snack items. Fruit bars, dried fruit, nuts, malt balls, corn nuts, sesame sticks, candy, chocolate bars, cheese, and nut butters are other favorite snacks. Sometimes I tuck in candy corn at Halloween or jelly beans at Easter. I try to balance texture and taste, providing variety in foods that are sweet-chewy, salty-crunchy, sweet-crunchy, salty-chewy, and so on.

Trail wisdom: You have to be open minded when planning food for a group. Not everyone will like the same foods that you do and vice versa. Don't forget your spice kit, a.k.a. food repair kit! Seasonings are key ingredients to successful meals. Plan ahead to make meals as easy to prepare as possible. Plan on taking more food than you think you will need. Carrying it can be a pain, but we have found that food stress caused by shortages can create morale problems that really affect the overall quality of a backpacking trip. Staying well-fed and hydrated are key components of a successful wilderness experience.

Cinnamon Rolls

What a way to greet the day!

At home, pack in a plastic bag and tie off:

⅓ cup raisins
⅓ cup chopped walnuts
¼ cup brown sugar
3 tablespoons butter powder

In rest of bag, pack:

1 ¾ cup store-bought biscuit mix
¼ cup sugar

On trail, pour all but ¼ cup biscuit mix into a pot or bowl and add:

¼ cup plus 2 tablespoons water

Stir well, adding reserved biscuit mix as necessary. Dough should be soft but not sticky. Turn out onto a clean, flat surface. (A piece of closed-cell foam covered with duct tape makes a lightweight cutting board and work surface.) Knead a few times, adding more biscuit mix as necessary.

Form into a rectangle 6 inches by 8 inches and about ½ inch thick. Sprinkle filling on dough, making sure filling goes almost to edges. Roll dough jelly-roll style so that the dough forms a log. Cut into pieces 1 inch thick.

For a *boil-in-a-bag type baker (5½ inches in diameter),* using half the recipe, bake/boil in an oven bag 15 minutes or until done and let stand 3 minutes.

For a *boil-in-a-bag type baker (7½ inches in diameter),* bake/boil in an oven bag 25 minutes or until done and let stand 5 minutes.

For a *convection-oven type baker (6 or 7 inches in diameter),* bring thermometer into bake zone and then bake 20 to 22 minutes or until done.

For a *convection-oven type baker (8 inches in diameter),* bring thermometer into bake zone and then bake 18 to 20 minutes or until done.

Servings: Full recipe makes about 8 cinnamon rolls.
Nutritional information: 476 calories, 13 grams fat, 78 grams carbohydrate, and 9 grams protein per 2 rolls.

**Mmmm good!
For a lightweight cutting
board and work surface, cover
a rectangle of closed-cell
foam with duct tape.**

Variation: Cinnamon Rolls in Backpacking Dutch Oven

If the cinnamon roll mix rises too high in a backpacking Dutch oven, it will get too near the lid and burn. For a 7-inch-diameter pan, use this slightly smaller recipe:

On trail, follow the above instructions for Cinnamon Rolls, reserving only 2 tablespoons biscuit and adding to the biscuit/sugar mix:

    3 tablespoons water

Form into a rectangle 5 or 6 inches by 7 inches and about ½ inch thick. After sprinkling on the topping and making the roll, cut into pieces ¾ inch thick. Bake 18 to 20 minutes or until done.

Servings: Makes 8 small cinnamon rolls.
Nutritional information: 286 calories, 9 grams fat, 43 grams carbohydrate, and 6 grams protein per 2 rolls.

At home, pack together:
¼ cup raisins
¼ cup chopped walnuts
2 tablespoons brown sugar
2 tablespoons butter powder

Pack separately:
**1 cup plus 2 tablespoons
    biscuit mix**
2½ tablespoons white sugar

Grits, Eggs, and Bacon

This recipe isn't a hot cereal, and it isn't a bread, and it doesn't come from the frying pan. It's a casserole, which is something that generally doesn't appear on trail. Nonetheless, here it is, full of bacon and eggs and grits to tickle your fancy. And the bonus is—no clean-up.

If your cupboard is bare of bacon morsels or imitation bacon morsels, substitute salad sprinkles, which are surprisingly good.

To double the recipe, pack and cook the eggs separately (6 tablespoons powdered eggs to ¾ cup water) and then add to the cooked grits mixture (1½ cups instant grits, ¼ cup bacon morsels, 2 tablespoons powdered milk cooked up with 2 cups boiling water). Or, if you have a boil-in-a-bag type baker, put all ingredients in a medium or large oven bag. Increase cooking time to 15 minutes, or more, until done.

Want to spice it up? Try adding cheddar cheese, hot sauce, Tabasco, salsa, or other condiment of choice.

■

At home, combine and mix well in a small oven bag:

¾ cup (two 1-ounce packets) grits

3 tablespoons powdered eggs

2 tablespoons bacon or imitation bacon morsels

1 tablespoon powdered milk pinch paprika

On trail, add:

1 cup minus ½ tablespoon water.

Mix well. Leave a small amount of air in the bag and tie the bag closed. Place bag as horizontally as possible in a pot with about 1½ inches of boiling water. Cover pot and turn down stove so water simmers. Cook casserole for 10 minutes. Add salt and pepper to taste. (Some brands of instant grits have salt added, so check the taste before you add more.)

Servings: Makes one serving of a little more than 1½ cups.
Nutritional information: 399 calories, 11 grams fat, 46 grams carbohydrate, and 20 grams protein.

CHAPTER 4

Lunch and Snacks

Before starting I donned heavy flannels, woolen hose, warm mittens and goggles, blacked my face with charcoal to modify the sun's glare, drove long caulks and brads into my shoes, rolled two single blankets containing provisions for three days and strapped them from the shoulder under the arm to the waist, the easiest way by far to carry a pack, shouldered one of Uncle Sam's canteens, grasped my alpenstock and was resolved to climb until exhausted. . . . Among us we had dried beef, fried ham, cold boiled eggs, sardines, bread and butter, extract of beef, cheese, chocolate, dried peaches, raisins and prunes.

Fay Fuller, the first woman to climb Mount Rainier, "A Trip to the Summit," in *Every Sunday*, 1890

©Jeff Scher

For backpackers lunch is a process, not an occasion, and each individual approaches it in a different way. Some stuff in energy bars and keep walking. Others carry a more traditional variety of crackers, nut butters, dried fruit, cheese, and other snacks. And still others enjoy tabouli salad, couscous salad, and other rehydratable meals. Most take a modular approach to lunch, packing foods that can be eaten in short stops throughout the day. In fact, nutritionists advise snacking on carbohydrates every hour or hour and a half to replenish your glycogen, which muscles need for hard work.

One way to look at lunch and snack foods is to sort them into nutritional categories. Hikers should draw from each category, with a greater emphasis on complex carbohydrates, but should not ignore fats, which provide energy for the long haul:

Simple carbohydrates: Jam, dried or fresh fruit, fruit leather, fruit cookies and bars, candy.

Complex carbohydrates: Bready foods like bagels, tortillas, pita bread, and crackers; pretzels; energy bars (depending on brand); salads like tabouli and couscous.

Protein-rich foods: Jerky; tuna and sardines (if packed in water these are low in fat); cheese and salami (both also contain fat).

Fat-rich foods: Cheese, salami, nuts, nut and seed butters, coconut, chocolate.

Another way to sort through lunch offerings is by their taste and texture. (If you haven't already read Claudia Pearson's suggestions for making lunch interesting, check them out on page 63.) The categories could be something like this: Salty and chewy foods—jerky, dulce (seaweed). Salty and crunchy foods—pretzels, crackers, nuts. Sweet and chewy foods—dried fruit and fruit leather, licorice. Sweet and crunchy foods—granola bars, animal crackers. And so on until you've exhausted the wide range of foods that can be eaten between breakfast and dinner.

Karen Berger's Hot Tips

Karen has hiked the Appalachian Trail, the Continental Divide from Mexico to Canada, the Arizona Trail, and the Pyrenees High Route. She is a contributing editor to *BACKPACKER.* Her latest book is *Everyday Wisdom: 1001 Expert Tips for Hikers.*

Style: I backpack for weeks or months at a time, so I don't have the time or energy to do anything fancy with food. It's a question of weight and storage—plus I don't have any energy left at the end of the day.

Lunch standbys: For lunch, I eat a lot of cheese because of the high fat content. I read articles that say it's not a good idea to get so many calories from fat, but I think to myself,

"They're not long-distance hikers." I have used dried hummus and instant refried beans, and they are good for a change. Tiny cans of sardines or smoked oysters are a wonderful treat. Otherwise I rely on pemmican-type bars, jerky, and fruit leather.

Trail dinners: If I'm carrying up to five days of food, I use supermarket food—spaghetti, macaroni and cheese, dried potatoes and a can of salmon, Parmesan and rice, and soups. If I'm carrying food for six to ten days, I go with freeze-dried or very lightweight food. For a fifteen-day stretch, I use all freeze-dried food with maybe some of the Lipton-type pasta dinners that cook very quickly.

GORP, DRIED FRUIT MIXES, AND OTHER SNACKS ••••••••••

Gorp and snacks of dried fruit and nuts are a potent way to carry calories. Nuts are high in fat and dried fruit is condensed and therefore more concentrated than fresh. Beware of ingredients like chocolate bits and yogurt-covered raisins that melt when the temperature goes up, leaving you with a gooey residue on plastic bag and fingers.

Tropical Mix

The fruit and nuts provide the base flavor and the ginger provides the snap.

Servings: Makes four servings of a little more than ½ cup each.
Nutritional information: 203 calories, 11 grams fat, 24 grams carbohydrate, and 9 grams protein.

At home, combine:
½ cup dried papaya
½ cup dried pineapple
½ cup coconut
½ cup cashews
⅓ cup candied ginger
  (or to taste)

Bedouin Gorp

The fruit of the date palm, which has long sustained Bedouins crossing the desert, is important in Arabian cuisine. *Tamr bil Simsim,* for example, is an Arabian confection made by combining chopped dates with cardamom, almonds, and ground pistachios, shredded coconut, or sesame seeds. These ingredients also make a simple but intriguing gorp. I don't include sesame seeds because they tend to settle to the bottom of the bag, and no one wants them when everything else is gone.

If possible, use dates and shredded coconut without added sugar, because the dates themselves provide enough sweetness. The cardamom, which will adhere to the cut dates, lends a subtle undertone.

At home, combine:
½ cup chopped dates
½ cup shredded coconut
½ cup sliced almonds
½ cup pistachios
⅛ teaspoon ground
  cardamom

Servings: Makes four servings of ½ cup each.
Nutritional information: 276 calories, 21 grams fat, 27 grams carbohydrate, and 6 grams protein.

Garden Gorp

OK, we're moving a long way from good old raisins and peanuts here. Combine tomatoes, peppers, corn, and peas—with a crunchy salad topping—in this unusual snack. But before you put together a batch, test the tomato flakes and bell pepper flakes to see whether the ones you have are edible in their unrehydrated state.

■

At home, combine:
½ cup freeze-dried peas
½ cup freeze-dried corn
½ cup tomato bits or flakes
½ cup dried bell pepper
¼ cup salad sprinkles

Servings: Makes four servings of a little more than ½ cup each.
Nutritional information: 130 calories, 4 grams fat, 20 grams carbohydrate, and 7 grams protein.

Raisins and Candied Ginger

Sometimes less is more. Instead of tossing everything into one big bag of gorp, consider making several separate gorps, providing something a little different each day and making the most of particularly flavorful combinations. Candied ginger, for example, dances with flavor. Team it up with raisins, and you have a zingy blend. Look for candied ginger in the supermarket spice section or buy it in bulk at a health food store. Chocolate lovers may want to add 1 cup chocolate bits.

■

At home, pack:
⅓ cup diced candied ginger
    (or to taste)
2 cups raisins

Servings: Makes four servings of slightly more than ½ cup each, or, with chocolate bits, six servings.
Nutritional information: 147 calories, 0 grams fat, 36 grams carbohydrate, and 0 grams protein; with chocolate bits, 233 calories, 8 grams fat, 43 grams carbohydrate, and 1 gram protein.

Apricots and Cranberries

This combo has, as Martha Stewart would say, presentation appeal. The golden-orange apricots and bright red cranberries just beg you to take a handful.

■

At home, pack:
1 cup dried apricots
1 cup dried cranberries

Servings: Makes four servings of ½ cup each.
Nutritional information: 207 calories, 0 grams fat, 51 grams carbohydrate, and 0 grams protein.

Ilo's Fruit Leather

Fruit leather is great on bagels, tortillas, and pita bread. Ilo Gassoway also recommends spreading fruit leather with cream cheese—regular or flavored—and then rolling it up into a little jelly roll. It's guaranteed to keep you going for a few more miles.

When you make fruit leather you can experiment with flavors and textures. Ilo's favorites are apple-strawberry and apple-pineapple-coconut.

At home directions continued, spread the mixture ⅛ to ¼ inch thick on a non-stick cookie sheet or dehydrator tray covered with plastic wrap (see Chapter 2 for tips on drying). Dry at 130 to 135 degrees until the mixture is leathery. Drying can take anywhere from 8 to 20 hours, depending on the thickness of the mixture, the humidity, and other factors. Remove from tray, cut into individual portions, roll in plastic wrap or waxed paper, and store in a plastic bag in a cool, dry, dark place.

Servings: Makes 15 pieces of fruit leather.
Nutritional information: 55 calories, 0 grams fat, 13 grams carbohydrate, and trace grams protein per piece.

■

At home, purée in blender:
16 ounces strawberries or mixed berries

Then add:
24 ounces applesauce
3 tablespoons thawed orange juice concentrate
water as needed

Cranberry-Orange Leather

Initially, I made and dehydrated a batch of cranberry-orange relish to use as a side dish for a Thanksgiving-in-July meal. The relish was vibrant—the tart cranberries complemented the zesty orange bits, shouting "This tastes like fresh food!" at every bite. The relish went over well, but how often does one have Thanksgiving in July? I needed another way to present this great combo, so I made it up as a fruit leather, and it's been a hit ever since. Friends who have used this recipe say that they've put small pieces of leather into both tea and hot cereal to sweeten and flavor it.

Because cranberries are a seasonal fruit, I whip up several big batches in the late fall and dip into the stash as long as it lasts.

At home directions continued, stir well. Spread on non-stick cookie sheet or a dehydrator tray covered with plastic wrap. Dry at about 135 degrees until it is leathery (see Chapter 2 for drying tips for sauces) but not brittle. Store in a cool, dark, dry place.

Servings: Makes about 3 cups relish or about 10 servings fruit leather.
Nutritional information: Using 1 cup sugar, 102 calories, trace grams fat, 66 grams carbohydrate, and 1 gram protein.

■

At home, rinse and pick over:
4 cups (1 bag) cranberries

Rinse and cut into medium-small pieces:
1 orange with skin

Then put the cranberries and orange chunks through a food processor. Place in a bowl and add:
¾ to 1 cup sugar, depending on desired sweetness

Mincemeat Bars

It is almost as easy to make mincemeat bars as it is to buy prepackaged bars. Buy a box of condensed mincemeat, slice into bars of individual portion size, bag, and refrigerate. On trail, be sure to drink plenty of water—condensed mincemeat is concentrated stuff.

Servings: A 9-ounce box will yield 4½ servings of 2 ounces each.
Nutritional information: 200 calories, 1 gram fat, 48 grams carbohydrate, and trace grams protein.

Bank Balls

Joe Bank, a staffer at Rodale Press (*BACKPACKER's* parent company), enlisted the aid of Rodale nutritionist and registered dietitian Anita Hirsch to come up with a recipe for an alternative to store-bought energy bars. They developed a snack that has lots of carbos as well as nutrients like thiamin (B-1), niacin, riboflavin, and potassium. These bars or balls, depending on how you make them, don't melt on hot days or break your teeth on cold days, and the cost is minimal compared to energy bars, which run $1.00 or more.

Hirsch warns that if you chow down on a lot of these balls, the high fiber content may cause stomach distress, so—as with all foods— eat them in moderation until you see how your body reacts.

At home, combine in a food processor and chop into fine bits:
24 dried figs
⅓ cup honey
¼ cup orange juice
2 tablespoons lemon juice

In a large bowl, combine:
2½ cups unbleached flour
½ teaspoon baking soda
½ teaspoon baking powder
1 tablespoon canola oil
2 egg whites
¼ cup dark corn syrup
1 teaspoon lemon juice

At home directions continued, stir well (3 to 4 minutes at medium speed with an electric mixer) and then add the fig mixture, continuing until all ingredients are well mixed. Make 20 balls, roll them in oat bran, bake at 350 degrees for 10 minutes or until they are a somewhat puffy, and then chill in refrigerator. For a chewier texture, bake a total of 12 to 15 minutes. To make squares instead of balls, sprinkle oat bran on a greased cake pan, pat the dough into a square, and then sprinkle on the remaining oat bran.

Servings: Makes 20 servings of one ball each.
Nutritional information: 135 calories, 1 gram fat, 31 grams carbohydrate, and 2 grams protein per ball.

Savory Trail Mix

For an elegant and tasty snack, try this trail mix created by Janice Coom, chef at Green Valley Spa in St. George, Utah. It's a winner!

At home, preheat oven to 375 degrees. Cut in 1-inch cubes:
2 cups sourdough bread

Drizzle with:
1 teaspoon olive oil

Place on baking sheet and bake about 15 minutes, stirring several times. Remove when bread is crisp and slightly browned. While bread is baking, brown in a frying pan over medium heat until seeds begin to pop:
¼ cup hulled pumpkin seeds

At home directions continued, in a large bowl, mix the bread, seeds, and the following ingredients:

> **1 tablespoon freshly grated Parmesan cheese**
> **1¼ cups mini pretzels**
> **3 tablespoons shelled pistachios**
> **3 tablespoons roasted peanuts**
> **2 cups vegetable crisps (see recipe, below)**
> **fresh pepper (to taste)**

Store in plastic bags.

Servings: Makes twelve servings of H cup each.
Nutritionl information: Approximately 95 calories, 5 grams fat, 12 grams carbohydrate, and 3 grams protein.

Spiced Vegetable Crisps

With all the peeling, this recipe takes some time to make but it's well worth the effort. Kosher salt and sea salt are larger-grained than regular table salt. Although the larger grains are nice here, you can substitute table salt.

If the crisps loose their crispiness because of high humidity, not to worry. The spicy vegetable pieces will still taste great.

At home, peel:
6 medium carrots
1 sweet potato

Using a peeler, make long, thin strips or curls, keeping the carrots and potato separate. Drizzle onto the vegetables (half on each pile) and then rub in with your hands:

> **1 teaspoon olive oil**

At home directions continued, mix together:

> **1 teaspoon kosher salt or sea salt**
> **1½ teaspoons ground cumin**
> **¾ teaspoon ground coriander**
> **pinch cayenne pepper**
> **fresh pepper (to taste)**

Sprinkle half the seasoning mixture on the carrots and the remainder on the sweet potato. Place the two vegetables on separate cookie sheets and bake at 375 degrees, stirring every 3 to 4 minutes. Bake the carrots for about 20 minutes and the sweet potato about 30 minutes. They should be crisp and brown but not burned. Let cool and store in plastic bag.

Servings: Makes eight servings of ½ cup each.
Nutritional information: Approximately 60 calories, 1 gram fat, 12 grams carbohydrate, and 1 gram protein.

BREADS ·

Bready foods are a major source of complex carbohydrates. But although dried fruit, nuts, and dehydrated goodies are relatively impervious to mold, the critical question with bready food is: Once free of a refrigerator's life-support system, how long will your lunch munchie last against the encroaching fuzzy green stuff? The answer, of course, varies with the water content of the food in question as well as your traveling and camping conditions. Bone-dry foods last longer than those with moisture, and hot, humid weather makes mold go wild, while cool, dry weather keeps it in check.

In an at-home test, *BACKPACKER* food editor Jim Gorman carried individually packaged bagels, whole wheat pita, corn tortillas, and pilot biscuits in his gym bag—through all kinds of temperature and humidity conditions—to see how they fared. The result: Mold appeared in seven days on bagels, nine days on pita, seven weeks on corn tortillas, and not at all on pilot biscuits.

My own more anecdotal experience is that I can count on bagels for about five days, flour tortillas for about a week, and crackers indefinitely (crumbling is a bigger issue than mold), depending on conditions.

At about 250 calories each, bagels are the work horses of trail breakfasts and snacks. There are lots of options—garlic, onion, and pumpernickel for savory spreads or raisin-cinnamon for sweet spreads. Although tortillas have only 150 calories, and pita breads only 120 calories (for 7- to 8-inch diameter breads) both can take savory or sweet, lots and lots of it, certainly more than you could heap on a bagel.

Crackers can last surprisingly well if they are packed carefully. Empty Pringles-type cans and well-cleaned quart milk containers work nicely for cracker storage. Crisp flatbreads like lavash or Scandinavian flatbrød keep indefinitely and also last well if similarly protected.

▲ ▲ ▲

Trail-baked Lunch Breads

If you are willing to wield a pancake flipper, you can whip up some quick lunch breads during breakfast. For bannock, use a supermarket biscuit mix or make your own from a standard biscuit recipe. On trail, add water so it's somewhere between the consistency of pancake batter and biscuit batter—in other words, so it is thicker than runny but not stiff. Pan bake (fry with very little oil) on one side and then flip over and pan bake on the other. Bannock should be thicker than pancakes but not as thick as biscuits. One cup biscuit mix plus about ⅓ cup water will yield 6 pieces of bannock.

Another option is pancake cornbread. Use an off-the-shelf mix, add water so the batter is a bit stiffer than the consistency of pancakes, and cooks 'em up. The mix I use calls for the addition of milk and an egg. Add the appropriate amount of powdered milk (⅓ cup dry to 1 cup liquid) when you are packing. You can add powdered egg or egg replacer, or you can punt—with acceptable results—and use the mix without.

Muffin mixes can be used in the same way, though they do need some extra leavening (1 teaspoon baking powder or 2 teaspoons powdered egg per 1 cup mix). Both cornbread and muffin pancakes take time to cook, so the technique is better suited to one or two people rather than a larger group, unless you're planning on spending the morning cooking.

SPREADS ·

Where would hikers be without peanut butter and jelly? Peanut butter provides fat (read: lots of calories) and jelly provides simple carbohydrates (read: quick energy). It's a combo that works, trip after trip. Other nut butters, like cashew butter, walnut butter, and almond butter, are delicious—if more expensive—additions to the backcountry larder. Cheese, cream cheese, sardines, hummus, black bean spread, and refried beans—the latter three from dry mixes—are also trail standbys.

Mail order companies now offer salad spread mixes to enliven your lunch. When combined with olive oil, za'atar, a Middle Eastern spice blend, makes an unusual backcountry spread for pita bread. Or, with black bean spread or refries, cheese, and dehydrated salsa, you can have your own little Mexican meal.

The French have long used chocolate spread on toasted slices of baguette—an image that evokes the aroma of fresh bread, the chewiness of toast, and the luscious taste of smooth chocolate. If the thought appeals, then check your local store for chocolate hazelnut spread and be the envy of the power lunch crowd.

If your tastes take you still farther afield (sorry for the pun), give the following spreads a try.

Quick Curried Hummus*

To boost the calorie count, add a teaspoon of olive oil or ½ teaspoon powdered shortening.

At home, combine:
¼ **cup minus 1 teaspoon hummus mix**
½ **teaspoon curry powder**

On trail, add:
¼ **cup water (or more to achieve desired consistency)**

Servings: Makes one serving of ¼ cup spread.
Nutritional information: 110 calories, 4 grams fat, 15 grams carbohydrate, and 6 grams protein.

Curried Hummus with Veggies*

If you want something with a little more zing, try the following recipe. Lemon juice and olive oil contribute to the flavor, but this spread does well without. The coconut adds fat, which enhances the overall effect.

On trail, put dry ingredients in a small container with a watertight lid and add:

> ¼ cup boiling water

Mix well, cover, and let stand 10 minutes. Add salt, olive oil, and lemon juice to taste. Put cover on container and carry until you're ready for a snack. Good on bagels, crackers, and tortillas.

Servings: Makes one serving of ¼ cup spread.
Nutritional information: With the olive oil, 129 calories, 7 grams fat, 14 grams carbohydrate, and 3 grams protein.

■

At home, combine:
1½ tablespoons dried
  hummus
1 tablespoon dried cabbage
½ tablespoon tomato bits or
  flakes
1 teaspoon tomato powder
1 teaspoon coconut cream
  powder or powdered coconut
½ teaspoon dried onion
⅛ teaspoon garlic powder
¼ teaspoon curry powder

Carry with you:
1 or 2 packets lemon juice
  (optional)
about ½ teaspoon olive oil
  (optional)
salt

Tomato and Toasted Almond Spread*

Toasting the almonds gives this spread a rich, deep flavor. (See page 113 for tip on how to toast nuts.)

On trail, add:

> 2 tablespoons boiling water

and let stand 10 minutes or add cold water and let the spread rehydrate until lunch.

Servings: Makes one serving of ¼ cup.
Nutritional information: 76 calories, 6 grams fat, 4 grams carbohydrate, and 3 grams protein.

■

At home, combine:
2 tablespoons toasted, finely
  chopped almonds
2 tablespoons tomato bits or
  flakes
1⁄16 teaspoon dried basil
pinch garlic powder
salt to taste

Turkey Salad Spread*

Chicken, crab, egg, tuna, and beef salad spreads are making their way into the backcountry in the form of dry mixes packaged with packets of mayonnaise, relish, and other ingredients. Enterprising trail cooks can make their own versions by using freeze-dried turkey, chicken, tuna, or beef and adding dried vegetables, seasonings, and mayonnaise.

What follows is a basic recipe that you can tinker with to match your own tastes. It's written for turkey, but any other freeze-dried meat or seafood will work. When choosing vegetables, pick ones like tomato flakes and bell pepper flakes that will rehydrate in cold water in 5 minutes. (Mixed red and green bell pepper flakes are a nice choice because they add variety and color to the salad.) Celery, a regular addition to lunch salad spreads, will not rehydrate quickly enough unless during preparation you put it in a blender and chop it into very small pieces.

A packet or two of relish will also add variety, if you choose not to use the wasabi (horseradish) powder or mustard. See page 45 for tips about using mayonnaise in the backcountry.

■

At home, combine:

⅔ cup (1 ounce) freeze-dried turkey

¼ cup vegetables (for example, 2 tablespoons tomato flakes and 2 tablespoons mixed bell pepper flakes)

¹⁄₁₆ teaspoon garlic powder

⅓ teaspoon wasabi or dried mustard or to taste (optional)

Also pack:

3 tablespoons mayonnaise (in small packets)

On trail, mix dry ingredients with:

1 cup minus 1 tablespoon cold water

or enough water to barely cover the dry ingredients. Stir well and let stand 5 minutes. Drain water if there is extra. Add mayonnaise, salt, and pepper to taste.

Servings: Makes two servings of almost ½ cup each or one serving of almost 1 cup.

Nutritional information: 801 calories, 41 grams fat, 39 grams carbohydrate, and 12 grams protein per recipe.

Tomato Spread*

This spread is quick and easy. You can use a commercial mix of to-mato bits, Parmesan cheese, and seasonings, or make your own from scratch.

On trail, add:

3 tablespoons boiling water

and let stand 10 minutes or add cold water and let the spread rehy-drate until lunch.

Servings: Makes one serving of about ¼ cup.
Nutritional information: 95 calories, 7 grams fat, 3 grams carbohy-drate, and 4 grams protein.

At home, combine:
2 tablespoons tomato bits or flakes
1 tablespoon grated Parmesan cheese
1 teaspoon dried onion
1 teaspoon dried bell pepper
½ teaspoon mixed oregano, basil, thyme, and rosemary
¼ teaspoon garlic powder
⅛ teaspoon salt (or to taste)

Dill-Garlic Spread*

This spread is powerful with a sharp bite of garlic.

On trail, mix with:

2 tablespoons water

Servings: Makes one serving of 2 tablespoons.
Nutritional information: 96 calories, 10 grams fat, 2 grams carbohy-drate, and trace grams fat.

At home, combine:
2 tablespoons butter powder
2 tablespoons dill
2 teaspoons onion powder
1 teaspoon garlic powder
dash salt

Cheese and Garlic Spread*

If you want the taste of cheese but you don't want to deal with a chunk of grease on a hot day, try this spread (which does not, how-ever, have as many calories as does real cheese).

On trail, start with:

1 tablespoon water

and add more as needed to reach desired consistency.

Servings: Makes one serving of about 2 tablespoons.
Nutritional information: 152 calories, 9 grams fat, 6 grams carbohy-drate, and 6 grams protein.

At home, pack:
¼ cup cheese powder
¾ teaspoon garlic powder

REHYDRATABLE VEGETABLES AND SALADS ••••••••••••••••••

A bowl with a snap-on lid not only holds heat in when you're making no-cook dinners, it's useful when you want to rehydrate ingredients preparatory to a meal. For each of the following salads, all you have to do is add water at breakfast and let the ingredients rehydrate until you're ready to dig in at lunch.

Almond-Tomato Couscous Salad*

Almonds and tomatoes are a great combo.

■
At home, combine:
1/4 cup couscous
3 tablespoons toasted almonds, chopped fine
3 tablespoons tomato bits or flakes
1/4 teaspoon dried basil
1/8 teaspoon garlic powder

On trail, combine dry ingredients with:
> 1/2 cup plus 2 tablespoons boiling water

Let stand for 10 minutes, then add salt and pepper to taste. Carry in a container with a secure lid.

Servings: Makes one serving of approximately 1 1/3 cups.
Nutritional information: 279 calories, 9 grams fat, 41 grams carbohydrate, and 11 grams protein.

Sanna's Wheat Salad*

This recipe incorporates an off-the-shelf dry mix sold variously as tabouli or Middle Eastern wheat salad with fresh vegetables to make a meal that works perfectly in the desert. Because you have to carry water (and fresh vegetables provide water), it's not as though you're carrying extra weight. Instead of drinking water, you're getting liquid through the food itself.

■
At home, combine:
3/4 cup bulgur from tabouli mix
seasonings from spice packet

Pack separately:
3 or 4 scallions or one Kirby (small pickling) cucumber
1 carrot
4 sprigs parsley
2 tablespoons lemon juice (optional)
2 tablespoons olive oil

On trail, at breakfast chop the vegetables and put all ingredients in a plastic bowl with a secure lid and add:
> 1 cup cold water

The mix takes about 1 hour to rehydrate.

Servings: Makes one serving of about 3 3/4 cups or two servings of almost 2 cups each.
Nutritional information: 720 calories, 14 grams fat, 109 grams carbohydrate, and 13 grams protein per recipe.

Why *Not* Carry a Cucumber in the Desert?
Compare:
  a cucumber (regular size, not Kirby) that weighs ½ pound is 96 percent water and has about 30 calories, 1 gram fat, 10 grams carbohydrate, 1 gram protein, small amounts of vitamins and minerals, and a refreshing flavor.
  a cup of water weighs ½ pound and has no calories or other nutrients.

Bean and Pasta Salad*

One- or two-person packets of salad dressing go well with this salad. Or, carry an olive oil-based Italian dressing that does not need to be refrigerated.

On trail, place dry ingredients in a container and add:
  1½ cups boiling water
Cover and let stand 10 minutes or until rehydrated. Drain water. If you are using a non-refrigerated dressing, add it now and let the flavors mix with the salad; otherwise, add the dressing at lunch.

Servings: Makes one serving of 2 cups or two servings of 1 cup each.
Nutritional information: 392 calories, 16 grams fat, 52 grams carbohydrate, and 11 grams protein per recipe.

At home, combine:
½ cup freeze-dried kidney beans
¼ cup no-cook (no-boil) pasta or Chinese noodles
2 tablespoons dried carrots or other dried veggies
2 tablespoons dried onion

Pack separately:
1 or more tablespoons salad dressing

OTHER LUNCH MUNCHIES ····

Alan's Spicy Teriyaki Turkey Jerky

When I went to see Alan Kesselheim and Marypat Zitzer give a slide show about one of their fourteen-month trips in Canada, someone from the audience asked, "What did you eat?" Alan answered, "Well, we ate normal food." In addition to grains and other foods, they had dried an immense pile of fruit, vegetables, and even whole meals ahead of time, then dined quite well on the trail. This is Alan's recipe for turkey jerky.

Very important: Poultry absolutely must be cooked before it can be dried into jerky.

■

At home, combine in a glass or ceramic (but not metal) bowl:

½ cup teriyaki sauce

½ cup soy sauce

¼ teaspoon fresh ground black pepper

pinch cayenne pepper (or to taste)

2½ pounds skinless, cooked turkey cut into ¼-inch slices

At home directions continued, cover and marinate overnight. Dry at 140 degrees until jerky is leathery and somewhat brittle. Let cool and store in a container in a cool, dark, dry place.

Servings: Makes 10 to 16 ounces of jerky, depending on dryness, or about 10 servings.

Nutritional information: 200 calories, 6 grams fat, 1 gram carbohydrate, and 32 grams protein.

Sun-dried Tomatoes

Yes, sun-dried tomatoes are great as snacks, either dried or rehydrated. If you are drying your own, sprinkle on a little salt and some herbs. The flavor concentrates when tomatoes are dried, so just a couple of tomato pieces pack a punch. Dried tomatoes are especially good with cheese on whole wheat pita bread.

Nutritional information: Per 5 pieces, 55 calories, less than 1 gram fat, 10 grams carbohydrate, and 3 grams protein.

Lunch usually includes a variety of munchies.

▲▲▲

Coleslaw

Coleslaw is good at lunch or as a side dish at dinner (see recipe on page 96). Add water to the veggies at breakfast and let them rehydrate until lunch, adding mayonnaise (if you are using it) just before you're ready to chow down. See page 45 for tips about using mayonnaise in the backcountry.

CHAPTER 5

Soups, Smoothies, and Side Dishes

If you want to be canny you will have somewhere in your own pack a modest supply of condensed soups and vegetables, a box or two of meat crackers, and three or four bottles of bouillon, to be brought out on occasions of famine. Anyway it is a comfort to know that you have provided against the wolf.
Grace Gallatin Seton, *A Woman Tenderfoot*, 1900

Hot drinks and soups can revive and restore. If the elements turn against you, consider stopping for a hot brew in the middle of the day. On cool-weather trips, a lightweight thermos with something hot for lunch can make a huge difference in attitude and fortitude. And a quick cup of something hot can set you up for getting camp chores done at the end of the day.

SOUPS • • • • • • • • • • • • • • •

Meriweather Lewis considered portable soup, a mixture of dried beans and vegetables, so important that he took almost two hundred pounds of it with him on his mission to explore the Louisiana Territory. But you don't have to be headed up the Missouri River to enjoy soup on trail, and you can probably get by with less than two hundred pounds.

John Harlin ©ERG

Pemmican Soup*

Pemmican is a traditional Native American food made of dried meat, dried fruit, and melted fat. Carried in a rawhide container called a parfleche, pemmican provided a sustaining food for long trips or for times when game was scarce.

Pemmican Soup combines the elements of pemmican in a delightful broth, the dominant flavor of which is the salty meat. Surprisingly, the apricots do not make the soup sweet but give it some body, while the butter powder provides an agreeable smoothness. See page 36 regarding dried beef.

■

At home, combine in a blender:

2 tablespoons diced dried
   apricots
¼ cup dried beef or jerky
   broken into pieces

Blend the two ingredients, then put them into a plastic bag with:
2 teaspoons butter powder

On trail, place the dry ingredients in an insulated cup or bowl and add:

   1 cup boiling water
Cover and let stand 10 minutes.

Servings: Makes one serving of 1 cup.
Nutritional information: 173 calories, 5 grams fat, 14 grams carbohydrate, and 16 grams protein.

Corn Chowder*

The tiny amount of bacon provides the traditional chowder taste and aroma, while the rehydrated vegetables give this dish lots of welcome texture. Oyster crackers, though optional, add texture. Pita bread or papadums are nice accompaniments. See page 36 regarding drying bacon.

■

At home, mix well, pack in a corner of a plastic bag, and tie off:

dash paprika
½ teaspoon parsley
1 teaspoon potato starch
3 tablespoons powdered milk
⅛ teaspoon salt
1 teaspoon butter powder

In the other corner, tie off:
about 20 oyster crackers

In the main part of the bag, pack:

2 teaspoons dried bacon
   morsels
1 tablespoon dried onions
1 tablespoon dried bell
   pepper
¼ cup instant hash browns
½ cup freeze-dried corn

On trail, place dehydrated and freeze-dried vegetables in an insulated mug or bowl and add:

   1¾ cups boiling water
Stir well, cover, and let stand 10 minutes. Next, stir the milk mixture into the chowder very slowly (to avoid creating lumps). Let stand for 2 more minutes. Add oyster crackers.

Servings: Makes one serving of 1¾ cups.
Nutritional information: 314 calories, 5 grams fat, 57 grams carbohydrate, and 12 grams protein.

Variation: Seafood Chowder*

Substitute a can of shrimp, ⅔ cup freeze-dried shrimp, or a can of crabmeat for the corn.

Nutritional information: Using canned shrimp, 324 calories, 4 grams fat, 40 grams carbohydrate, and 29 grams protein.

Instant Veggie Soup*

Use a combination of dried tomato bits or flakes, onions, green peppers, carrots, and other veggies to taste. Freeze-dried corn or freeze-dried peas are also good.

On trail, place soup mix in an insulated mug and add:
> 1 cup boiling water

Stir well, cover, and let stand for a few minutes. Add salt or soy sauce to taste.

Servings: Makes one serving of 1 cup.
Nutritional information: 36 calories, 0 grams fat, 7 grams carbohydrate, and 2 grams protein.

■

At home, blend in blender until you have powder and some small bits:
> ¼ cup dried tomato and veggies of choice

Cold Tomato-Veggie Soup*

Check out your local Mexican fast-food restaurant to see whether it has small packets of lemon juice (about 1 teaspoon each) as a condiment. If so, negotiate for a few packets to add zip to this backcountry dish. Or, put some lemon juice in a small, leakproof plastic bottle. (See page 125 for a tip about making your own tomato powder.)

On trail, put dry mix in a cup and add:
> 1 cup cold water

Stir well and let stand for 10 minutes. Add lemon juice.

Servings: Makes one serving of 1 cup.
Nutritional information: 58 calories, 0 grams fat, 13 grams carbohydrate, and 1 gram protein.

■

At home, combine:
> 1 recipe Instant Veggie Soup (above)
>
> 2 teaspoons tomato powder
>
> ½ teaspoon mixed Italian herbs (oregano, basil, garlic powder, thyme, rosemary)

Also pack:
> 1 teaspoon lemon juice

■
At home, mix well:
1 teaspoon bouillon powder
1 teaspoon potato starch
¼ teaspoon sugar

Add:
3 tablespoons dried sliced or
    broken shiitake mush-
    rooms, stems removed
2 tablespoons dried onion

Shiitake-Onion Soup*

The dried brown buttons of shiitakes may seem costly but their bold flavor and meaty texture add immeasurably to soups and stews. Because the stems are less flavorful, use only the caps.

On trail, place in insulated mug or bowl and add:
    1 cup boiling water
Cover and let stand 10 minutes.

Servings: Makes 1 serving of 1 cup.
Nutritional information: 67 calories, 1 gram fat, 16 grams carbohydrate, and 1 gram protein.

Variation: Shiitake-Rice Soup*

Substitute 2 tablespoons instant rice for the onion.

Nutritional information: 92 calories, 1 gram fat, 21 grams carbohydrate, and 2 grams protein.

Variation: Shiitake-Vegetable Soup*

Substitute 2 tablespoons quick-rehydrating vegetables (such as thinly cut strips of dried tomato, dried peppers, freeze-dried corn, or freeze-dried peas) for the onion.

Nutritional information: 56 calories, 1 gram fat, 14 grams carbohydrate, and 1 gram protein.

▲ ▲ ▲
Comparison Shopping for Shiitake Mushrooms

You can save money by buying in quantity, and buying pieces rather than whole mushrooms. Compare:

At Chinese market: $4.89 for 3 ounces sliced dried mushrooms ($1.63/ounce)

At local supermarket: $2.99 for ¾ ounce whole mushrooms ($11.66/ounce)

In addition, whole mushrooms must be cut into thin slices to rehydrate quickly enough for instant meals, whereas many dried pieces will be thin and brittle enough to snap into the right size thickness. Because the stems of shiitake mushrooms are less flavorful than the caps, remember to remove and discard the stems first.

Sweet Carrot Soup*

Crunchy carrots give this soup great texture, an element that is so often missing in instant backcountry fare.

On trail, place mixture in an insulated cup and add:
    1 cup boiling water
Mix well, cover, and let stand 10 minutes. Salt to taste.

Servings: Makes one serving of 1 cup.
Nutritional information: 82 calories, 0 grams fat, 21 grams carbohydrate, and 0 grams protein.

At home, combine:
¼ cup thinly sliced or
    shredded dried carrots
1 teaspoon dried onion
1 teaspoon potato starch
1 tablespoon plus 1 teaspoon
    orange powder
dash cinnamon
dash nutmeg
dash mace
salt to taste

Variation: Savory Carrot Soup*

If sweet soup doesn't appeal, try this savory version. Follow the above recipe except omit the orange powder, cinnamon, nutmeg, and mace. Add instead: 1 teaspoon powdered milk, ½ teaspoon bouillon powder, and ½ teaspoon dill.

Nutritional information: 39 calories, 1 gram fat, 8 grams carbohydrate, and 1 gram protein.

Noodle Soup*

This soup can be made as is or with dried vegetables added to taste.

On trail, place in an insulated mug and add:
    1 cup boiling water
Cover and let stand 10 minutes.

Servings: Makes one serving of 1 cup.
Nutritional information: For basic soup, 105 calories, 1 gram fat, 23 grams carbohydrate, and 3 grams protein.

At home, combine:
1 teaspoon bouillon powder
¼ cup crushed Chinese
    noodles
dried veggies (optional)

BACKWOODS SMOOTHIES ....

Backwoods smoothies are rich, thick, and creamy but—let the reader beware—very different in texture and taste than at-home smoothies, which rely on chilled fresh fruit. Some of these trail smoothies are thick enough to need a spoon, so keep one handy.

Hot Piña Colada Smoothie*

This recipe teams an off-the-shelf piña colada mix with powdered milk to make a very sweet smoothie that tastes a lot like dessert.

At home, combine and mix well:
1 envelope instant piña
   colada mix
⅓ cup powdered milk

On trail, place dry mixture in a cup and add:
   1 cup boiling water
Stir well.

Servings: Makes one serving of 1 cup.
Nutritional information: 220 calories, 0 grams fat, 43 grams carbohydrate, and 8 grams protein.

Hot Coconut Smoothie*

The coconut gives this hot drink some fat calories to keep your taste buds happy. If you are a real sugar hound, add more sugar to taste. For a Hot Ginger-Coconut Smoothie, add ½ teaspoon powdered ginger to the dry mix.

At home, combine:
¼ cup powdered milk
1 tablespoon coconut cream
   powder or powdered
   coconut
1 teaspoon sugar

On trail, place dry mixture in cup and add:
   1 cup boiling water
Stir well.

Servings: Makes one serving of 1 cup.
Nutritional information: 172 calories, 10 grams fat, 15 grams carbohydrate, and 7 grams protein.

Hot Almond Smoothie*

Almond paste is composed of ground almonds and sugar. Like its sibling, marzipan (which contains more sugar), it's incredibly rich. In the smoothie featured here, 38 percent of the calories come from fat, and in the variation that follows, a whopping 44 percent come from fat—and that's a lot of calories. I've given the recipe for a full cup, but you may find that half a cup is plenty.

This recipe is equally good—and quite refreshing—as a cold drink.

Although almond paste is expensive, when bought in a larger amount (say, a pound or more rather than 7 or 8 ounces), there are economies of scale. And it does taste so good.

On trail, place ingredients in a container with a lid and add:
   1 cup water (hot or cold)
Shake vigorously.

Servings: Makes one serving of 1 cup or two servings of ½ cup each.
Nutritional information: 439 calories, 22 grams fat, 61 grams carbohydrate, and 18 grams protein per cup.

■
At home, place in a blender and blend well:
½ cup powdered milk
¼ cup (2 ounces) almond paste
1 tablespoon plus 1 teaspoon sugar

Variation: Homemade Almond Paste Smoothie*

If the cost of almond paste is daunting, you can concoct your own version from almonds and sugar. The resulting paste has a grainier texture because the almonds aren't ground as completely, and unless you use blanched almonds, there will be lots of little brown flecks floating (harmlessly) in your mug. A few drops of almond extract help boost the flavor. If you add the extract to the sugar, and then add the sugar to the blender, the extract won't simply adhere to the bottom or sides of the blender. When blending, make sure that the almonds are ground as small as possible in order to impart an even consistency to the final product.

On trail, add:
   1 cup water (hot or cold)
Shake vigorously.

Servings: Makes one serving of 1 cup or two servings of ½ cup each.
Nutritional information: 662 calories, 33 grams fat, 71 grams carbohydrate, and 24 grams protein per cup.

■
At home, combine in a blender and blend very well:
½ cup powdered milk
½ cup almonds
¼ cup sugar
¼ teaspoon almond extract

Hot Chocolate Smoothie*

My goal in this recipe was to come up with an instant pudding that has pudding texture without the artificial taste that seems to come with commercial instant puddings. I didn't succeed entirely but came close. This recipe makes a rich, chocolaty, thick beverage, one that you're more likely to eat with a spoon than drink from your cup.

At home, mix well:
1 tablespoon plus 1 teaspoon sugar
1 tablespoon plus 1 teaspoon cocoa powder
¼ cup powdered milk
1 tablespoon plus 1 teaspoon potato starch

On trail, place dry ingredients in an insulated mug and add:
    1 cup boiling water
Mix well. Cover and let stand 5 minutes.

Servings: Makes one serving of 1 cup.
Nutritional information: 177 calories, 1 gram fat, 37 grams carbohydrate, and 7 grams protein.

Hot Fruit Smoothie*

The recipe includes orange powder, which gives the drink a wonderful zesty flavor, and potato starch, which thickens the smoothie and gives it some body.

At home, mix thoroughly:
2 teaspoons sugar
4 teaspoons potato starch
⅛ teaspoon salt
¼ cup orange powder

Put into blender 1 cup dried fruit, such as:
¼ cup raisins
4 pitted dates
4 dried apricots
2 pieces dried apple
2 halves dried peach
2 halves dried pear
and blend until the fruit is cut up into very small pieces and mixed well.

Pack into 4 individual servings, using:
1½ tablespoons dry ingredients
¼ cup blended fruit mixture per portion.

On trail, place 1 serving in mug and add:
    1 cup boiling water
Stir well, cover, and let stand 10 minutes.

Servings: Recipe makes four servings of 1 cup each.
Nutritional information: 206 calories, 1 gram fat, 54 grams carbohydrate, and 1 gram protein.

SIDE DISHES ••••••••••••••••••

BREAD AND CRACKERS

Breads are full of carbohydrates that refuel your body and replenish the glycogen you need for energy. Plus, they taste good and add texture to one-pot meals. The cornbread included here is especially easy to make.

Cornbread in a Bag

Fresh cornbread on trail, with no pots to clean. Can it be true? Yes! This baked-in-a-bag cornbread is simple and slick. The mix I use is quite sweet, almost a dessert, but it goes down fine anytime. The following recipe is based on a mix that contains about 1½ cups dry ingredients and calls for 1 egg and ⅓ cup milk, but it should work with other mixes with similar proportions.

If you want a quantity larger than that provided by this recipe, see pages 150–51 and substitute cornbread mix for cake mix, adding powdered milk proportionately.

At home, combine in a small oven bag:

¾ **cup cornbread mix**
2 **teaspoons powdered eggs**
1 **tablespoon powdered milk**

On trail, add:

¼ **cup water**

and mix well. Close bag, leaving a little air inside, and tie it shut, using the tie that comes with the bag. Press the batter-filled bag into a round shape the size of the pot. Place in a pot with about 1½ inches boiling water, cover, and boil for 10 minutes at medium heat. The water should be boiling harder than a simmer but less than a rolling boil. Remove from heat and let stand 3 minutes, then cut open bag and release steam.

Servings: Each bag makes one cornbread round about 1¼ inches high and 5½ inches in diameter.
Nutritional information: 546 calories, 14 grams fat, 91 grams carbohydrate, and 10 grams protein per recipe.

Variation: Bacon Cornbread

Add 1 tablespoon dried bacon or imitation bacon bits to the dry mix.

Nutritional information: 576 calories, 16 grams fat, 91 grams carbohydrate, and 13 grams protein per recipe.

Cindy Ross' Hot Tips

Cindy, who has hiked the Appalachian Trail and the Pacific Crest Trail, is now hiking with Todd Gladfelter (her husband), their small children, and llamas. Her latest book, written with Todd, is *Kids in the Wild: A Family Guide to Outdoor Recreation.*

Style: I am a combination of all three styles of cooking and usually combine all three in a trip, depending on the conditions. Because my husband and I travel with small children, who often need attention and get hungry quicker than adults, I'm not really into laborious, complicated meals that take a long time to prepare. The kids can't wait. I like a few freeze-dried, no-cook meals for killer days when we pull into camp late. We buy some grocery store foods like pasta and dried corn and incorporate them into our menu. I do some dehydrating—although I used to be a fanatic over it years ago. I even dried grapes to make raisins and had to cut each blasted grape in half so it would dry. Nowadays, I only dry specific foods.

Standbys: We purchase a fat-free spaghetti sauce and dry it on solid trays in our dehydrator. It reconstitutes very quickly and it's difficult to tell the difference from fresh—and I am an Italian. It is marvelous. We used to carry a packet of herbs and a can of tomato paste, which is heavier than dried sauce, and it still wasn't as good.

We dry meat—our children love it. You can get about 99 percent fat-free lean meat at the butcher now that leaves practically no grease residue after it's dried.

We usually carry a BakePacker and mix up our own cornbread recipe and apple cake (made with our dried apple bits). We use the recipe provided with the baker and adjust it to suit our taste. Warm bread, freshly baked, and lots of margarine is super out there.

For lunch, anything covered with mustard is a real big hit with our whole family. My kids put it on the three-foot-long beef sticks we usually carry, also on cheese, crackers, jerky, and bread. Bryce, my son, was even putting it on granola bars after two months on the trail because, of all the food in the lunch bag, it had the most flavor. If we have pretzels, the kids dip those in too. You can get mustard in a plastic squeeze bottle or buy fancy flavors and put them into little plastic bottles, preferably open-mouth for easy dipping.

Favorite recipes: Hash Browns with Jello (page 58), Fried Bread with Cinnamon and Sugar (page 60), Fried Garlic Bread (page 93), and Shepherd's Pie (page 118).

Fried Garlic Bread

Cindy Ross reports that fried garlic bread, made with a durable loaf, is a special addition to an Italian meal. "We fry buttered bread with a little garlic powder (not garlic salt) and a sprinkle of oregano if we have it." Her husband, Todd, made this on their first hiking date and so impressed Cindy that she decided he was a keeper!

Nutritional information: Using 1 slice of bread and 1 teaspoon butter, margarine, or oil, about 103 calories, 5 grams fat, 13 grams carbohydrate, and 3 grams protein.

Focaccia

If you want to impress your hiking partners, whip up this flat Italian loaf loaded with potent flavor. Focaccia is a yeast bread, so it takes a little longer to make, but the aroma of fresh bread is a great stimulant to the appetite.

On trail, make up the crust per pizza instructions. While it rises, add boiling water to garlic and onion, let stand 10 minutes (or until onions are rehydrated), and drain; mix in herbs. When bread is ready to bake, brush on olive oil and sprinkle on the onion and herbs.

For a *backpacking Dutch oven (7 inches in diameter),* bake 20 to 25 minutes until done.

For a *boil-in-a-bag type baker (5½ inches in diameter),* using half the recipe at a time, bake/boil 12 to 14 minutes and let stand 3 minutes.

For a *boil-in-a-bag type baker (7½ inches in diameter),* boil/bake 15 minutes and let stand 5 minutes.

For a *convection-oven type baker,* bake for 20 to 25 minutes or until done.

Servings: Makes four wedges.
Nutritional information: 255 calories, 14 grams fat, 34 grams carbohydrate, and 3 grams protein per wedge.

■

At home, make the crust recipe for pizza (see page 134). In another bag, pack:
1 teaspoon Italian herbs or a mixture of oregano, basil, and other herbs to taste
½ teaspoon garlic powder

Tie off these herbs and in the rest of the bag pack:
1½ teaspoons dried onion

Also, pack:
1 tablespoon olive oil, or add that amount to the oil that you are already carrying

Quick Pan-Baked Flatbread

This recipe is designed for the minimal backcountry kitchen—all you need is a pan (or pot) and a lid. The dough is the consistency of bread dough and bakes into a flatbread that tastes like whole wheat Syrian bread, or pita bread, but without the pocket. This flatbread should be eaten promptly, when it is still warm and the aroma of fresh bread lingers; it is especially good with chowder.

At home, combine, mix well, and place in a plastic bag:

¼ cup whole wheat flour
½ teaspoon brown sugar
¼ teaspoon baking powder
¹⁄₁₆ teaspoon salt
½ teaspoon olive oil
1 tablespoon finely chopped
   nuts

On trail, add:

   1½ tablespoons water

Stir until all liquid is absorbed, then knead the bag briefly by squeezing it in one hand, then the other, about 20 times. Let dough rest 3 minutes, then squeeze dough into a disk about ⅛ inch thick and 4½ inches in diameter. The dough will be slightly thicker than a tortilla. Pan bake by placing in a lightly greased, covered pan over moderate heat. (You can also use a pot, though it will be harder to turn the flatbread.) *Note:* Be careful that the flatbread does not burn. When one side is browned, flip it over and brown the other side. The bread will need about 2 to 2½ minutes per side, but the exact time depends on your stove.

Servings: Makes one serving.
Nutritional information: 179 calories, 11 grams fat, 25 grams carbohydrate, and 2 grams protein.

Tomato Pones

A pone is a cornmeal cake that is baked, fried, or boiled. These crispy tomato pones, which are more tomato than cornmeal, complement a chowder or stew. Use either a commercially prepared combination of tomato bits and other vegetables with seasonings, or make your own (see the recipe for Tomato Spread, page 79).

On trail, add to the dry mix:

5 tablespoons plus 1 teaspoon boiling water

Mix well and let stand several minutes. Make into thin, 3-inch round patties. Fry on one side 2 to 3 minutes or until golden brown, then fry on the other side.

Servings: Makes two servings of 2 pones each or one serving of 4 pones.

Nutritional information: 69 calories, 3 grams fat, 10 grams carbohydrate, and 2 grams protein per 2 pones.

■

At home, combine:
¼ cup tomato bits or flakes with seasonings
2 tablespoons cornmeal

Also pack:
1 teaspoon oil

Papadums

Papadums are large, thin "crackers" traditionally eaten with Indian food; they are made of lentil flour, rice flour, salt, oil, and leavening. I use them often at home to provide texture when I'm serving a one-pot meal like stew or soup, whether it's of Indian origin or not.

Look for papadums in the ethnic section of the supermarket. The ones my local store carries are about 4½ inches in diameter. The directions say to fry them in deep fat or brush with oil and cook them in a microwave oven. As they cook, papadums expand and crinkle, producing a crunchy texture much like that of potato chips. Test one at home (if you use the microwave method, you don't have to brush it with oil as the directions state) so you know what the final product looks like. When you get out on trail, skip the brushing with oil and "bake" them quickly over a moderately hot flame in a frying pan with a lid. The pan should be hot enough to cook the papadums in 45 to 90 seconds but not to burn them.

The papadums may get broken into pieces in your pack, but it doesn't matter because they'll still expand into chips. At three papadums to an ounce, you get a lot of flavor and texture for very little weight.

Servings: Serve one or two per person.

Nutritional information: Not including frying oil, 27 calories, 0 grams fat, 4 grams carbohydrate, and 2 grams protein per papadum.

SIDE DISHES • • • • • • • • • • • • • • • • • •

VEGETABLES

These dishes offer variety rather than calories, but when your taste buds are begging for change, variety counts for a lot. Besides, the ingredients are lightweight and the recipes are a snap to prepare.

Stewed Tomatoes*

You may not chow down on canned tomatoes at home but remember that dried tomatoes concentrate flavor and are oh-so-good on trail.

At home, pack:
6 pieces thinly sliced dried tomato
1½ teaspoons dried onion
1½ teaspoons dried bell pepper
⅛ teaspoon basil
⅛ teaspoon oregano
dash of garlic powder

On trail, place in insulated bowl or cup and add:
⅔ cup boiling water
Cover and let stand 10 minutes.

Servings: Makes one serving of ⅔ cup.
Nutritional information: 76 calories, 1 gram fat, 14 grams carbohydrate, and 4 grams protein.

Coleslaw*

Why go to the effort of carrying carrots and cabbage? Because they give you "fresh food" taste and crunch and they take the edge off food fantasies. You can hardly lose by giving coleslaw a try. (See page 45 for more about mayonnaise in the backcountry.)

At home, combine:
¼ cup dried cabbage (equal to 1 cup fresh shredded cabbage)
2 tablespoons shredded dried carrots
⅛ teaspoon caraway seeds

If you want a dressing, pack along small mayonnaise packets to taste. A small amount of vinaigrette is also good, as is a squirt of lemon juice and a dollop of olive oil.

On trail, place ingredients in an insulated bowl or cup and cover with boiling water. Cover container and let stand 10 minutes. Drain and let cool. Add dressing, if desired, and season to taste with salt and pepper.

As an alternative, if you have the time, add cold water and let the veggies stand an hour or more.

Servings: Makes one serving of ⅓ cup.
Nutritional information: With 1 teaspoon mayonnaise, 57 calories, 6 grams fat, 6 grams carbohydrate, and 1 gram protein.

Carrots with Salad Sprinkles*

Salad sprinkles (you can substitute toasted sesame seeds) add crunch while the butter powder adds a subtle flavor in this easy side dish. This recipe makes enough for two. If you're going alone, just cut the ingredients in half.

On trail, place carrots in an insulated bowl and add:
   1 cup boiling water
Cover and let stand 10 minutes. Drain the water and add the other ingredients.

Servings: Makes two servings of ½ cup each.
Nutritional information: 34 calories, 1 grams fat, 6 grams carbohydrate, and 1 gram protein.

■
At home, place in a plastic bag:
1 teaspoon butter powder
1 tablespoon salad sprinkles
   or toasted sesame seeds

Tie off these ingredients and then add:
½ cup thinly sliced dried
   carrots

Buttered Corn with Curry or Turmeric*

Buttered corn is delectable just as it is, but folding in a touch of curry powder or turmeric adds a hint of the Far East.

On trail, place corn in an insulated bowl and add:
   1 cup boiling water
Cover and let stand 10 minutes. Drain the water and add the other ingredients.

Servings: Makes two servings of ½ cup each.
Nutritional information: 88 calories, 2 grams fat, 17 grams carbohydrate, and 3 grams protein.

■
At home, place in a plastic bag:
1 teaspoon butter powder
generous pinch curry powder
   or turmeric

Tie off these ingredients and then add:
1 cup freeze-dried corn

■

At home, combine in a plastic bag and tie off:
½ teaspoon sugar

To the rest of the bag, add:
½ cup dried shredded cabbage
3 dried apple rings, diced

In a separate container, carry:
1 tablespoon lemon juice or rice wine

In your spice kit, carry Tabasco or hot sauce (or, add a few drops—to taste—to the lemon juice or rice wine).

Apple and Cabbage Salad*

What this recipe lacks is color (not a problem when dinner is in the dark, or if you're still wearing your sunglasses), but if you're drying your own cabbage, try the red variety to brighten up this otherwise interesting side dish that can be eaten hot or cold.

On trail, place cabbage and apple in an insulated bowl and add:
1 cup boiling water
Cover and let stand 10 minutes, then drain. Add the sugar, lemon juice or rice wine, and fiery stuff to taste.

Servings: Makes two servings of ½ cup each.
Nutritional information: 40 calories, trace grams fat, 11 grams carbohydrate, and 1 gram protein.

Variation: Bacon, Apple and Cabbage Salad*

Add 1 tablespoon dried bacon or imitation bacon morsels and ¼ teaspoon caraway or celery seed per serving. See page 36 regarding drying bacon.

Nutritional information: 55 calories, 1 gram fat, 11 grams carbohydrate, and 3 grams protein.

CHAPTER 6

Dinner

*Just bread and water and delightful toil is all I need—
not unreasonably much, yet one ought to be trained and tem-
pered to enjoy life in these brave wilds in full independence of
any particular kind of nourishment.*

John Muir, *My First Summer in the Sierra*, 1911

Your feet hurt, your back is tired, and you are getting just a tiny bit water-logged from the daylong drizzle when you drag into camp. There is everything to do: Change out of those damp and sweaty clothes, set up a tarp, set up the tent, store your gear, filter a few quarts of water, arrange your camp kitchen, and prepare dinner. Common sense tells you to eat something right away, even if it's just a snack left over from lunch, but you'd really like a hot meal in the very near future.

Dinner needn't take hours. No-cook dinners shine on days like this. You can calmly boil a few cups of water, let your meal soak 10 minutes, and chow down with little delay. There are more than thirty no-cook entrées here, along with some traditional and not-so-traditional entrées that require cooking. And if you get into camp extra early—or have planned a layover day—there's always the backpacker's dream food—pizza.

Most of the entrée recipes make one serving, and the calorie counts of some are clearly not enough to satisfy a hearty appetite. If you are a big eater, check the amount per serving and the nutritional information, and if the portion size seems too small or the calorie count too low double the ingredients or add a side dish and dessert.

©Jeff Scher

NOODLES ·····················

The recipes in this section all call for Chinese noodles (the kind used in ramen-type soups) or curly Japanese noodles, which are essentially the same thing. These noodles cook up nicely using the add-boiling-water-only method. Although most pasta turns to mush when cooked too long, Chinese noodles have some latitude, and soaking a minute more or less won't spell disaster.

Szechuan Veggie Noodles*

If peanut butter for dinner sounds unappealing, remember that Szechuan peanut sauce doesn't taste like peanuts. The nut butter blends with the bouillon, garlic, and ginger to produce a new, unusual, and rich flavor.

At home, combine:
¾ cup Chinese noodles
2 tablespoons dried cabbage
2 tablespoons thinly sliced
   dried mushrooms
3 tablespoons chopped,
   toasted cashews
1 tablespoon powdered milk
1½ teaspoons dried onion
1 teaspoon bouillon powder
¼ teaspoon ground ginger
⅛ teaspoon garlic powder

Pack separately:
1 tablespoon peanut butter

On trail, place all ingredients in an insulated bowl, stir well, and add:
   1½ cups boiling water
Stir well once more, cover, and let stand 10 minutes. Add salt or soy sauce to taste.

Servings: Makes one serving of a little more than 1½ cups.
Nutritional information: 591 calories, 10 grams fat, 88 grams carbohydrate, and 30 grams protein.

Ilo's Backpack Sukiyaki

Ilo Gassoway provided these hints on drying tofu: slice a block of firm tofu into ¼-inch thick pieces, freeze for at least 8 hours, then dry 6 to 12 hours at 140 to 145 degrees until the pieces are cracker-like. To prepare this recipe, he slices green onions, carrots, mushrooms, and celery to ¼-inch thickness and then dries these as well as a handful of bean sprouts along with the tofu.

Ilo uses homemade beef jerky in his Backpack Sukiyaki, but here I've teamed up his recipe with Spicy Teriyaki Turkey Jerky (see page 82). You can also use dried ground beef; stir in a teaspoon of soy sauce, a pinch black pepper, and a pinch cayenne pepper (or to taste) before drying the cooked beef.

In this recipe, you can substitute Chinese noodles, which don't come with a seasoning packet, for the rice thread or ramen noodles and add your own extra seasoning.

On trail, add vegetable and meat mixture to:

    3 cups boiling water

and simmer for 6 minutes. Add noodles and seasoning and cook for another 2 to 4 minutes, depending on the type of noodles. When noodles are done, add additional soy sauce if necessary. Best eaten with chopsticks!

Servings: Makes two servings of 2 cups each or four servings of 1 cup each.

Nutritional information: Approximately 516 calories, 7 grams fat, 80 grams carbohydrate, and 32 grams protein per 2 cups.

At *home,* pack together:

6 ounces dried tofu

4 strips Spicy Teriyaki Turkey Jerky, cut into pieces

¼ cup dried celery

In another bag, pack:

¼ cup dried bean sprouts

2 tablespoons dried green onions

¼ cup thinly sliced dried carrots

3-ounce packet of rice thread or ramen noodles

seasoning packet that comes with noodles or seasoning of choice

individual packets of soy sauce to taste

Variation: Instant Backpack Sukiyaki*

If you cut the tofu and vegetables so that they are ⅛ inch thick, or buy dried veggies that rehydrate (starting with boiling water) in 10 minutes, you can make an instant version of Ilo's recipe. Pack all ingredients in one bag, except seasonings and soy sauce. Place tofu, veggies, and noodles in an insulated bowl and add:

    3 cups boiling water

Stir, cover, and let stand 10 minutes. Add seasonings.

Beef Stroganoff*

Beef Stroganoff, which is served over rice or fettucine, is traditionally made with filet of beef, mushrooms, onions, sour cream, and a pinch of nutmeg. Dried ground beef, dried mushrooms, and dried onions are surprisingly good substitutes in the backcountry. If you don't have sour cream powder on hand, you can substitute one or two individually portioned packets of cream cheese; add after the stroganoff has cooked. I've called for Chinese noodles, but you can also use instant rice.

On trail, place beef mixture in an insulated bowl and add:
> 1 cup plus 2 tablespoons boiling water

Cover and let stand 10 minutes. Drain off (and drink, if you like) the broth. Add nutmeg and sour cream powder or cream cheese and mix well.

Servings: Makes one serving of about 1⅔ cups.
Nutritional information: With cream cheese, 397 calories, 10 grams fat, 69 grams carbohydrate, and 12 grams protein.

■

At home, place in the corner of a plastic bag and tie off:

1½ tablespoons sour cream powder or several packets cream cheese

pinch nutmeg

In the rest of the bag, place:

3 tablespoons dried ground beef

3 tablespoons thinly sliced dried mushrooms

¼ teaspoon dried chopped onion

⅔ cup Chinese noodles

Chinese Noodles and Veggies*

I've tried using angel hair pasta in instant dinners, but it passes through the *al dente* stage so quickly that it effectively goes from uncooked to unappealingly paste-like in the amount of time needed to rehydrate the other ingredients. Noodles allow some latitude with timing and are a better choice. Don't pour off the broth; it's tasty and will help you rehydrate. This dish is good with a bit of Parmesan cheese.

On trail, place ingredients in an insulated bowl and add:
> 3 cups boiling water

Turn off heat, cover, and let stand for 10 minutes. Add soy sauce to taste.

Servings: Makes one serving of 1½ cups.
Nutritional information: 447 calories, 0 grams fat, 104 grams carbohydrate, and 11 grams protein.

■

At home, combine:

2 ounces (1 cup) Chinese or curly Japanese noodles

½ cup dehydrated mixed vegetables

Also pack:

soy sauce to taste

Tunaless Noodle Casserole*

Your pack may further crush the corn chips called for here, but the pieces will still provide a contrast to the creamy texture of this casserole.

On trail, place all dry ingredients except corn chips in an insulated bowl and add:

> 1⅓ cups boiling water

Stir well, cover, and let stand 10 minutes. Add Worcestershire sauce, if desired, and stir. Sprinkle the crushed corn chips on top of the "casserole."

Servings: Makes one serving of about 1½ cups.
Nutritional information: 438 calories, 11 grams fat, 87 grams carbohydrate, and 12 grams protein.

At home, put in a plastic bag and tie off:

> 2 tablespoons corn chips, crushed

In the rest of the bag, combine:

> ⅔ cup Chinese noodles
> 1½ tablespoons freeze-dried peas (optional)
> 1 tablespoon thinly sliced dried mushrooms
> 3 tablespoons from package of dehydrated mushroom soup (or a little less than the amount required for 1 cup soup)
> 2 teaspoons dried parsley

If you carry Worcestershire sauce in your spice kit, use a dash when the meal is prepared, but if you don't, there is lots of flavor without.

Variation: Tuna Noodle Casserole*

Carry along one small can (3 ounces) of tuna and combine with dry ingredients before you add the boiling water, or pack ⅓ cup freeze-dried tuna with dry ingredients and add 3 extra tablespoons boiling water for rehydration. Remember that the odor of freeze-dried tuna can permeate the plastic bag and may attract animals who have a nose for such things.

Servings: Makes one serving of a little more than 1¾ cups.
Nutritional information: Using tuna packed in water, 554 calories, 13 grams fat, 87 grams carbohydrate, and 35 grams protein.

Annie Getchell's Hot Tips

Annie is co-host of the Public Broadcasting System program *Anyplace Wild* and is a contributing editor at *BACKPACKER*. She wrote *The Essential Outdoor Gear Manual*.

Style: I guess I'm a pragmatic gourmet. What's unusual about my camp kitchen is that I prepare and enjoy exactly the same foods no matter where I am. Somewhere along the path, it occurred to me that "low-impact" isn't just for the backcountry—that the yearned-for simplicity of trail life can be a restorative part of each day. I spend a fair chunk of life on the road as well as in the backcountry, and a consistent diet definitely helps keep me anchored and in top form.

Cook kit: My cook kit is lean but generously sized to serve me and up to three compatriots. I save weight on gadgetry but make up the difference with a well-stocked pantry. I always take a medium-size stainless sauce pan/lid plus a two-cup melting pot. A group of four means adding a six-quart stainless water pot. I also include a trimmed-down wooden spoon, one ancient army spoon, and two pairs of chopsticks whittled from willow twigs.

Standbys: Staples in our kit include oats; basmati rice; buckwheat noodles; seaweeds like nori or arame; miso; dried shiitake, porcini, and chanterelle mushrooms; raisins, currants, lots of dried cranberries and peaches; toasted sesame and pumpkin seeds, pine nuts and other nuts, especially roasted almonds. I dry herbs, onions, leeks, peas, carrots, and squash from our garden harvest, plus whatever fruit is in season. Strawberries in the snow . . . mmmmm.

Fragrant corn tortillas are my favorite food by a long shot. Toasted with jam for breakfast. Sandwiched with peanut butter, sprouts, and hot sauce for lunch. Grilled quesadillas in camp. Broken stale remains browned in butter for chips or floated in soup.

Favorite recipes: One of my favorite recipes is Fried Seaweed and Soba, a.k.a. Spider Legs and Brains (see page 105).

Gadgets: We always pack a simple nylon tarp—100 percent worth its weight in rainy country. You can rig a kitchen tarp for a trailside tea break in the time it takes water to boil.

Gourmet tip: Purchase an assortment of petite, one-, two-, and four-ounce plastic containers for condiments. They're leakproof, they last for years, and they add considerably to your repertoire when filled with hot sauce, tamari, olive or sesame oil, mustard, conserves, what have you.

Packing tip: When you purchase grapes or onions, save the expandable netting bags. They make terrific organizers in your camp kitchen.

Annie's Fried Seaweed and Soba (a.k.a. Spider Legs and Brains)

Annie Getchell's favorite recipe makes a meal that is delicious hot or cold—Annie says it is especially good the next day for a cold lunch. If you're new to sea vegetables or are introducing them to someone else, this is a lovely initiation. Soba are traditional Japanese whole wheat/buckwheat noodles.

On trail, rinse seaweed (this is the "spider legs") and soak for several minutes to rehydrate; let any sandy sediment settle. Rehydrate vegetables if necessary; slice veggies if using fresh.

Prepare buckwheat noodles (these are the "brains"). These noodles cook quickly—*al dente* in about 7 minutes. Drain the noodles (save the water) and then sprinkle with a little of the sesame oil to keep them from sticking together in a giant wad.

Heat a few tablespoons of sesame oil in your skillet. Reduce heat to medium. Add onions and carrots first, then top with seaweed. Pour in a little soaking water to create steam. Cover and cook for several minutes; remove lid and stir before topping the vegetables with noodles. Cover and cook a few more minutes before stirring in Secret Sauce.

To make Secret Sauce, add to nut butter-miso mix:

⅓ to ½ cup reserved hot water from noodles

Add hot sauce to taste and thin with more water if necessary.

Servings: Makes two servings of about 2 cups per serving or four servings of 1 cup per serving.

Nutritional information: For one serving of 2 cups, about 575 calories, 31 grams fat, 92 grams carbohydrate, and 18 grams protein.

■

At home, pack these items separately:

8 ounces soba (buckwheat) noodles

½ cup arame (a type of seaweed)

2 to 3 tablespoons sesame oil

Also pack:

½ carrot or ¼ cup thinly sliced dried carrots

1 onion or leek (or amount to taste) or their dried counterparts

Also pack:

3 tablespoons almond or cashew butter

2 tablespoons miso paste

PASTA •

Pasta is great on trail, when my body wants to load up on carbos at the end of a hard day. If water and fuel are at a premium, I use recipes for no-cook meals, but if not, then I indulge myself.

Because both volume and weight are always considerations when loading a pack, I conducted an informal survey at the supermarket to discover which form of pasta comes in the most compact shape. Spaghetti and tiny pasta stars tied for first place, small elbow macaroni placed second, and small shells placed third.

Lemon Pepper Penne with Mushrooms

Whenever I run across a good "starting point" ingredient, I check out the package for recipes that I might be able to adapt for use in the backcountry. This recipe came about just that way, with thanks to the American Italian Pasta Company.

This recipe is equally good on regular or flavored pasta. So far, I've sampled pastas flavored with basil and garlic, porcini mushrooms, chili peppers, smoked salmon, tomato and basil, and lemon pepper. These pastas are an easy way to get new tastes into the trail menu. Of course, there are lots of convenience pasta-with-garlic-butter products on the supermarket shelves, but by making your own you can take advantage of the great varieties in pasta shape and taste.

At home, combine in a plastic bag and tie off:
1 tablespoon butter powder
¼ cup Parmesan cheese
⅛ teaspoon garlic powder

In another corner tie off:
¼ cup dried mushrooms, cut into large slices

In remainder of bag place:
¾ cup (4 ounces) lemon pepper penne

On trail, bring to a boil:
3 to 4 cups water

Add penne. Follow package directions for boiling time, stirring frequently to make sure pasta doesn't stick to the pot. Add the large mushroom pieces 4 or 5 minutes before the pasta is done. When pasta is *al dente*, remove from stove and pour off all liquid except ½ cup. (It may be easier to pour the liquid into a bowl, then add back ½ cup.) Stir in the dry ingredients. Add salt and pepper to taste.

Servings: Makes one serving of 1½ cups.
Nutritional information: 433 calories, 15 grams fat, 51 grams carbohydrate, and 20 grams protein.

Variation: Lemon Pepper Penne with Mushrooms and Shrimp

Pack along a 4-ounce can of water-packed shrimp or half a cup of freeze-dried shrimp. To rehydrate the shrimp, soak for a few minutes in water. Drain water from whichever type you use and add to pasta when you add the sauce ingredients.

Servings: Makes one serving of about 2 cups.
Nutritional information: 478 calories, 15 grams fat, 51 grams carbohydrate, and 30 grams protein.

▲ ▲ ▲

Pasta: Tips and Types

Pasta should be cooked *al dente* or "firm to the tooth." Pasta is undercooked when it is hard to chew and overcooked when it is entirely soft. It has cooked the proper time when the outside layer is soft and the inner layer offers slight resistance, thus providing texture.

Angel hair pasta and tiny star pasta take 2 to 4 minutes to cook. These two pastas need to be watched carefully because they can easily overcook and lose texture. Start testing at one minute and pour off the water as soon as they are *al dente*. These pastas are not good choices for instant meals because other ingredients may require more cooking time than does the pasta.

Using pasta of different shapes and flavors can add variety to your backcountry cuisine. Pictured here clockwise, starting upper left: orzo or rice-shaped pasta, lemon pepper penne, smoked salmon farfalle or bows, semolina penne, chili pepper linguine, moose-shaped pasta, small shells, roasted bell pepper and garlic rotini or spirals, medium shells, and (center) stellini or tiny stars.

Tomato Pasta with Spinach-Cheese Sauce

You can make the following dish with regular semolina-based pasta, but tomato pasta goes particularly well with the spinach sauce. *Note:* Tomato pasta is not enhanced by tomato sauce—too much of the same flavor.

■

At home, combine:

1½ tablespoons dried cream of spinach soup or spinach powder

3 tablespoons Parmesan cheese, grated

1½ tablespoons buttermilk powder or butter powder

1 tablespoon powdered milk

¼ teaspoon oregano

a few grains of cayenne pepper

Also pack:

¾ cup (3 ounces) tomato-flavored pasta

On trail, combine powdered ingredients with:

¼ cup boiling water

Let stand. Meanwhile, bring to boil:

3 to 4 cups of water

and add the pasta. Follow package directions for boiling time (according to the type of pasta used), stirring frequently to make sure pasta doesn't stick together or to the pot. When pasta is *al dente,* remove from the stove and pour off liquid. Combine with spinach-cheese sauce. If you are using spinach powder rather than soup mix, add salt and pepper to taste.

Servings: Makes one serving of 1½ cups.

Nutritional information: 555 calories, 23 grams fat, 78 grams carbohydrate, and 15 grams protein.

Chicken and Broccoli Shells

Turmeric is a spice from India that gives a golden color to everything it touches, including curry powder. Like its relative ginger, turmeric has an assertive flavor and so must be used with discretion. This recipe calls for just a pinch to brighten up an otherwise bland-looking meal. If visual appeal is not of interest, you can safely eliminate this ingredient.

■

At home, pack:

1 cup shells

2 tablespoons freeze-dried chicken

2 tablespoons freeze-dried broccoli

1 teaspoon dried onions

1 teaspoon chicken bouillon powder

1 teaspoon potato starch

1 teaspoon buttermilk powder (optional)

2 teaspoons powdered milk (3 if not using buttermilk)

⅛ teaspoon garlic powder

⅛ teaspoon parsley

pinch turmeric (optional)

On trail, bring to a boil:

2 cups water

Slowly add the ingredients, stirring frequently. Boil 9 to 10 minutes until the pasta is done. If the sauce becomes too thick or if there is not enough water for the pasta to continue cooking, add more water a tablespoon at a time.

Servings: Makes one serving of about 1¾ cups.

Nutritional information: 483 calories, 18 grams fat, 91 grams carbohydrate, and 7 grams protein.

No-cook Mac and Cheese*

Yes, you can buy a box of macaroni and cheese at the store for a nominal amount, but you can also make the mix yourself. For the instant version, use no-cook (no-boil) pasta.

On trail, make sure ingredients are well mixed. Place in insulated bowl and add:
    1 cup boiling water
Cover and let stand 10 minutes.

Servings: Makes one serving of 1½ cups.
Nutritional information: 492 calories, 15 grams fat, 84 grams carbohydrate, and 16 grams protein.

At home, pack:
¾ cup no-cook (no-boil) pasta
1½ tablespoons cheese powder
½ cup powdered milk
salt and pepper to taste

Variation: Mac and Cheese

If you want to use regular pasta, substitute ¾ cup macaroni or shells for the no-cook pasta. Pack milk and cheese powder together in another bag. On trail, boil pasta in 1 quart water, cooking until it is *al dente*. Drain all but ¼ cup water. Add milk-cheese powder slowly, stirring well so the powder does not lump. Cover and let stand 5 minutes. Add salt and pepper to taste.

Southwest Beans and Penne

The Italian penne adds some texture and bulk to these otherwise New World ingredients.

On trail, add ingredients to:
    1 cup plus 2 tablespoons boiling water
Simmer for 10 minutes or until penne is done, stirring occasionally. Add water if necessary so that there is enough water to cook the pasta.

Servings: Makes one serving of 1½ cups.
Nutritional information: 321 calories, 2 grams fat, 67 grams carbohydrate, and 10 grams protein.

At home, combine:
¾ cup penne
2 tablespoons freeze-dried black beans
1 tablespoon freeze-dried corn
1 tablespoon tomato bits or flakes
1 tablespoon tomato powder
1 teaspoon chicken bouillon powder
½ teaspoon dried onion
½ teaspoon chili powder
¼ teaspoon basil
¼ teaspoon cilantro
pinch garlic powder

COUSCOUS, BULGUR, AND GRITS ••••••••••••••••••••

Couscous, bulgur, and grits rehydrate almost instantly and are great in no-cook dishes. I've included only a few recipes using each, but it's easy to make up your own. Boxes of these ingredients often feature recipes that can be easily adapted for trail use.

Cheesy Couscous*

There are a lot of variations on the couscous theme—serve it with chicken, herbs, and butter; substitute freeze-dried peas and dried carrots for the tomatoes; mix in some fresh red bell pepper and (for a first night out) fresh broccoli. Let your taste buds guide your menu.

At home, combine:
½ cup couscous
6 pieces thinly sliced dried tomato

Add to the above mix:
2 tablespoons plus 1 teaspoon cheese powder

Or pack separately:
1 ounce (one 1-inch cube) cheddar cheese

On trail, if you are using cheese powder, make sure cheese is well mixed with couscous. Put dry mix in insulated cup or bowl and add:
1 cup boiling water
Cover and let stand 10 minutes. Add salt and pepper to taste. If you are using fresh cheese, slice and add just before eating.

Servings: Makes one serving of about 1¾ cups.
Nutritional information: Using cheese powder, 482 calories, 8 grams fat, 84 grams carbohydrate, and 20 grams protein; using fresh cheese, 483 calories, 6 grams fat, 81 grams carbohydrate, and 22 grams protein.

Grits and Veggies*

Grits, which are made from corn, are an excellent instant ingredient for those with an allergy to wheat. Others, of course, can enjoy grits, too. When made as directed, this dish is more soupy than solid, but there needs to be plenty of liquid for the mushrooms and grits to rehydrate fully. To make Blue Cheese Grits and Veggies, substitute blue cheese powder for the cheddar cheese powder.

On trail, place dry ingredients in an insulated bowl and add:
　　1½ cups boiling water
Stir well, cover, and let stand 10 minutes.

Servings: Makes one serving of 1½ cups.
Nutritional information: 329 calories, 9 grams fat, 51 grams carbohydrate, and 10 grams protein.

■
At home, combine:
¼ cup plus 2 tablespoons freeze-dried peas
¼ cup plus 2 tablespoons thinly sliced dried mushrooms
¼ cup plus 2 tablespoons (1 packet) instant grits
2 teaspoons butter powder
3 tablespoons cheddar cheese powder (or a slice or two of whole cheese)
dash paprika

▲ ▲ ▲

Most Popular Event

We find that a trip is more fun if we have a surprise party one evening of the trip. Even experienced backpackers forget from season to season how tired they get carrying a pack all day, and how exquisite the pain can be. Sure, you're in a beautiful spot and you're doing what you want to do, but as fatigue and soreness set in, you might feel just a little bit like you're on a forced march, and resolve that your next vacation will be spent at the beach. To alleviate that feeling and to revive that festive feeling we all had the first morning of the trip, we bring out the party favors and special snacks on the evening that we reach some objective on the trip. For favors we will have straws or picks festooned with Mylar fringes or foldout honeycomb paper fruit, which we'll slip into beverages or stick into pieces of cheese to signal that it's party time. We may not use these favors much at home, but we've never failed to have a few laughs with them in the backcountry.

—John Emelin

Buck's Couscous with Feta Cheese

This recipe from Buck O'Herin, which calls for fresh vegetables and feta cheese, is great for an evening early in the trip. Like many trail chefs, Buck cooks by feel, so I assigned some quantities for the seasonings as I scaled down the amounts to serve two. As with any recipe, adjust the seasonings to your own taste.

Buck dehydrates the green peas before he leaves and then rehydrates them on trail. You can pack frozen peas for the first night out or freeze-dried peas for a subsequent meal, though drying peas is really quite easy (see page 37).

If you like your dinners savory then skip the raisins, which add a subtle sweetness to this dish.

On trail, rehydrate dried peas and tomatoes by placing them in a pot and simmering in:

> **2 cups or more water**

After 10 minutes, add the raisins. (If you are using fresh or freeze-dried peas, add with the raisins.) Meanwhile, remove stem and seeds of red pepper and chop; mince fresh garlic; and peel and mince fresh ginger. When the peas, tomatoes, and raisins have rehydrated, place them in a bowl, saving the cooking water in the pot. Next, sauté the red pepper, ginger, and garlic in a frying pan. If you are using garlic powder and ground ginger, add them when the pepper is almost done. Add pea mixture to frying pan and set aside. Increase leftover cooking water to:

> **2 cups**

Bring to a boil and add couscous. Return to a boil, stir, cover, and take off the stove. Let stand for 10 minutes or until all of the water has been absorbed. Add contents of frying pan to couscous. Serve individual portions, adding feta cheese, salt, and pepper to taste.

Servings: Makes two 1½ cup portions.
Nutritional information: 725 calories, 8 grams fat, 110 grams carbohydrate, and 33 grams protein.

At home, pack:
1 cup couscous

In a separate bag, pack:
⅔ cup dried tomatoes
¼ cup dried or ½ cup fresh or freeze-dried peas

Also pack these fresh items:
1 fresh red bell pepper
⅓ cup raisins (optional)
¼ pound feta cheese
1 clove garlic (or garlic powder to taste)
3 slices fresh ginger (or ⅛ teaspoon ground ginger or to taste)

Carry in a leakproof container:
2 teaspoons oil

In your spice kit, include:
cayenne pepper
salt and pepper

Variation: Instant Couscous with Feta*

If you're not using fresh vegetables, try this variation—the sliced almonds add texture.

On trail, place contents of bag in insulated bowl and add:
   1 cup minus 1 tablespoon boiling water
Stir well, cover, and let stand 10 minutes. Stir in crumbled feta cheese and almonds. Add salt or soy sauce and pepper to taste.

Servings: With raisins, makes one serving of 1½ cups.
Nutritional information: With raisins, 382 calories, 10 grams fat, 58 grams carbohydrate, and 15 grams protein.

▲ ▲ ▲

Toasting nuts

To toast nuts, place them in a skillet with a few drops of oil over medium heat, or in a 350-degree oven for 10 or more minutes until they are lightly browned. The nuts will continue browning slightly after they have been removed.

At home, toast:
1 tablespoon sliced almonds

Let cool and tie off almonds in the corner of a plastic bag. Then combine these ingredients in the rest of the bag:
¼ cup couscous
¼ cup tomato bits or flakes, or thinly sliced dried tomatoes
1½ tablespoons dried red bell pepper
1½ tablespoons raisins (optional)
2 tablespoons freeze-dried peas
¹⁄₁₆ teaspoon garlic powder
¹⁄₁₆ teaspoon ground ginger
few grains of cayenne pepper

Pack separately:
1 ounce (one 1-inch cube) feta cheese

International Couscous*

This recipe brings couscous from northern Africa, almonds from the Mediterranean, chili from Mesoamerica and South America, and cranberries from New England together for a lively, quick meal.

On trail, place all ingredients except almonds in an insulated bowl and add:

> ½ cup plus 1½ tablespoons boiling water

Mix well, cover, and let stand 10 minutes. Add almonds.

Servings: Makes one serving of a little more than 1½ cups.
Nutritional information: 351 calories, 7 grams fat, 64 grams carbohydrate, and 11 grams protein.

■

At home, place in a plastic bag and tie off:

1½ tablespoons toasted sliced almonds

To the rest of the bag, add:

¼ cup plus 2 tablespoons couscous

2 teaspoons dried cranberries

2 teaspoons currants or raisins

2 teaspoons thinly sliced dried carrots

2 teaspoons dried onions

1½ teaspoons chicken bouillon powder

1½ teaspoons chili powder

½ teaspoon garlic powder

¼ teaspoon brown sugar

Easy Bulgur and Beans*

This meal is as easy to pack as it is to prepare, for it uses only four ingredients: a store-bought instant soup mix, bulgur, tomato bits or flakes, and a dash of chili powder. A slice of cheddar cheese, a few crushed corn chips sprinkled on top, or a dollop of salsa will add extra zip.

The point here is that you can get some great variety by using one-cup soup mixes as the basis for your entrée. Vegetable soup with bulgur or couscous and corn chowder with instant rice are but two of the possibilities. Look for any soup that "cooks" in 5 minutes with the addition of boiling water.

On trail, place dry ingredients in an insulated bowl and add:

> 1½ cups boiling water

Mix, cover, and let stand 10 minutes. Add salt to taste.

Servings: Makes one serving of a little more than 1½ cups.
Nutritional information: 407 calories, 2 grams fat, 87 grams carbohydrate, and 18 grams protein.

■

At home, combine:

¼ cup plus 2 tablespoons small-grained bulgur

dry ingredients from one 1-cup package instant black bean soup

2 tablespoons tomato bits or flakes

¼ teaspoon chili powder (or to taste)

Wheat Pilaf, Loaded*

For the "cream of . . ." soup mix in this recipe, I use spinach or cheddar and broccoli, but there are lots of dried soup options. Combine with veggies of your choice, as long as they are ones that will rehydrate in hot water in 10 minutes.

Look for salad sprinkles in the salad dressing and crouton section of your supermarket. There are various brands, which may or may not include sunflower seeds, sesame seeds, small bits of dried vegetables, and soy products. Adding the sprinkles just before eating means that you get a wonderful contrast in texture—fine-grained bulgur, chunky veggies, crunchy sprinkles, and creamy sauce.

On trail, place bulgur mixture in an insulated bowl and add:
  1 cup minus 1 tablespoon boiling water
Stir, cover, and let stand 10 minutes. Mix in salad sprinkles.

Servings: Makes one serving of 1⅔ cups.
Nutritional information: 344 calories, 4 grams fat, 68 grams carbohydrate, and 12 grams protein.

At home, add to a plastic bag and tie off:
  2 tablespoons salad sprinkles

In the rest of the bag, combine:
  ¼ cup plus 2 tablespoons
    small-grained bulgur
  ¼ cup mixed dried vegetables
  1 tablespoon powdered
    "cream of . . ." soup mix

Mark Jenkins' Hot Tips

Mark is the Rocky Mountain field editor for *BACKPACKER* and an investigative reporter for *Men's Health*. His latest book is *To Timbuktu: A Journey Down the Niger*, which describes the first descent of the Niger River headwaters in western Africa.

Style: I am a super-ascetic, opting for minimal prep and minimal cooking. I am also a complete omnivore; this includes the entire insect kingdom as well as mammalian viscera.

Standbys: Hot chocolate and dried apricots for breakfast, sardines or oysters for lunch, and the lightest, quickest pasta meal available for dinner. A particular favorite: sardines smothered in peanut butter.

Trail wisdom: For extreme adventures, I believe that meat is essential. Jerky, tuna, sardines—whatever. I feel that meat gives a bigger boost than any carbo meal and it lasts longer. Even the vegetarians I know, when in desperate circumstances, will hunger for meat.

To me, food and sleep are luxuries. The only essential is water (and love, of course).

Gadget: Insulated mug.

POTATOES ••••••••••••••••••••••

To many folks, spuds are comfort food, so they play to the psyche as well as the stomach. Instant mashed potatoes have long been an important ingredient in trail cuisine, and instant hash browns, a relative newcomer, are quickly elbowing their way into food packs.

Unstuffed Potatoes*

This recipe calls for peas, carrots, and bell peppers, but you can use any combination that you want; mushrooms, corn, and tomatoes, for example, are also good. You can use a commercial mixed veggie or garden veggie blend as long as all of the components will rehydrate in 10 minutes.

The following recipe makes up into relatively soft mashed potatoes, my theory being that extra water is always good for rehydration. If you like your potatoes firmer, then decrease slightly the amount of water you add to the powdered mix.

■

At home, place in a plastic bag and tie off:

2 tablespoons toasted, sliced almonds

In the rest of the bag, combine:

¼ cup powdered milk
1 tablespoon butter powder
½ cup instant mashed potatoes
2 tablespoons Parmesan cheese
¼ teaspoon garlic powder
dash salt or to taste

To make Unstuffed Wasabi Potatoes, add 2 to 3 teaspoons (or to taste) wasabi, a powdered horseradish. To make Stuffed Dilley Potatoes, add 1 tablespoon dill to the potato mix.

In another plastic bag, combine:

2 tablespoons freeze-dried peas
2 tablespoons thinly sliced dried carrots
1 tablespoon dried bell peppers

On trail, place powdered ingredients in a bowl (an insulated bowl will keep the food hotter) and add:

1 cup boiling water

Stir well, cover, and let stand 10 minutes. Meanwhile, add about:

⅔ cup boiling water

(or enough to cover the vegetables generously) to an insulated mug or to the plastic bag itself, as long as you insulate the bag. Let stand 10 minutes. Drain water from veggies and add veggies to potatoes. Top with toasted almonds.

Servings: Makes one serving of almost 1½ cups.
Nutritional information: 352 calories, 13 grams fat, 45 grams carbohydrate, 10 grams protein.

Variation: **Unstuffed Potatoes with Bacon***

Add 1 tablespoon dried crumbled bacon, low-fat bacon morsels, or a vegetarian equivalent (See page 36 regarding drying bacon.) If using bacon, store ingredients in refrigerator or freezer until your trip.

Nutritional information: 382 calories, 14 grams fat, 45 grams carbohydrate, and 13 grams protein.

Variation: **Unstuffed Potatoes with Fresh Veggies**

Substitute ⅔ cup fresh vegetables for the dehydrated vegetables. Steam separately from potatoes and combine when potatoes have rehydrated.

Nutritional information: 387 calories, 13 grams fat, 53 grams carbohydrate, and 18 grams protein per serving.

Basil Potatoes*

This recipe uses dried pesto that you can buy in an envelope in the supermarket. Although reconstituted store-bought pesto does not have as robust a flavor as fresh pesto, the dry version is easier to pack and it has a longer shelf life. The optional ½ tablespoon olive oil contributes to a smooth "mouthfeel."

On trail, place dried veggies in an insulated mug or bowl and cover generously with boiling water. Cover and let stand 10 minutes. Drain water except for about 2 teaspoons and add pine nuts, pesto, cheese, and—if desired—olive oil. Stir well.

Servings: Makes one serving of about 1½ cups.
Nutritional information: With oil, 385 calories, 15 grams fat, 53 grams carbohydrate, and 11 grams protein.

At home, combine in a plastic bag and tie off:
2 tablespoons toasted pine nuts
1 tablespoon from packet of dried pesto
1 tablespoon Parmesan cheese

In the rest of the bag, pack:
¾ cup instant hash browns
1 tablespoon thinly sliced dried mushrooms
1 tablespoon red bell peppers or tomato bits or flakes

Also carry:
½ tablespoon olive oil (optional)

Variation: **Basil-Bacon Potatoes***

Add 1 teaspoon dried bacon morsels to veggie mixture and store in refrigerator or freezer until trip.

Nutritional information: 415 calories, 17 grams fat, 53 grams carbohydrate, and 13 grams protein.

▲ ▲ ▲

Cindy's Shepherd's Pie

Cindy Ross' recipe for Shepherd's Pie is a classic "cup of this and cup of that." Writes Cindy: "We use loose, dried ground meat to make a shepherd's pie on the trail. I first rehydrate the meat by soaking it and cooking it a bit. Then let it stand. We also have dried corn soaking. We cook that, adding some powdered milk—Todd is a Pennsylvania German, and this is their traditional recipe. Then we add an envelope of instant gravy mix to the water in the meat and heat to thicken. Make the mashed potatoes according to the package, adding powdered milk, margarine, salt, and onion powder. When everything is done, the mashed potatoes go into your bowl first, then the corn, then the meat and gravy. This meal is the all-time favorite of everyone in our family. It is very filling, tastes like real food, and is relatively quick. It takes just two pots plus a lid that is used for the meat and gravy. Even if your timing is off, things can stand and wait. Make the potatoes last."

It's easy to adapt Cindy's directions to suit your own appetite. One cup water (more or less according to box directions) plus ¾ cup instant mashed potatoes, ¼ cup powdered milk, 1 teaspoon margarine, and seasonings makes about 1 cup potatoes. Use ¼ cup dried ground beef (from ½ cup ground beef) and ¼ cup dried corn (from ½ cup fresh or frozen). Put them all together with ¼ cup gravy (made from ¼ package gravy mix) and you have about 1¾ cups of Shepherd's Pie.

Nutritional information: For the amounts described above, 384 calories, 7 grams fat, 81 grams carbohydrate, and 20 grams protein.

Crustless Russian Vegetable Pie*

Russian (or Cossack) Vegetable Pie is a rich concoction of cream cheese, veggies, and hard-boiled eggs piled into a pie crust. Cookbooks that emphasize low-fat cooking tactfully omit this dish because it has so much fat; it also takes a long time to prepare. The following recipe preserves the flavor but leaves out the crust and long preparation time. If you are planning this meal for the first or second night out, consider taking along a hard-boiled egg to cube and mix into the vegetables. Pack along papadums, bread sticks, or some crunchy, bready food to serve as a counterbalance to this stew-type meal and to provide extra calories.

On trail, place dry ingredients in an insulated bowl and add:
   1½ cups boiling water
Stir well and make sure that all dried ingredients are covered. Cover bowl and let stand 10 minutes. Add bouillon, cream cheese, and—if desired—a hard-boiled egg that has been chopped into medium pieces. Stir well.

Servings: Without egg, makes one serving of about 1⅔ cups.
Nutritional information: Without egg, 265 calories, 14 grams fat, 32 grams carbohydrate, and 5 grams protein; with egg, 344 calories, 20 grams fat, 33 grams carbohydrate, and 11 grams protein.

At home, place in a plastic bag and tie off:
1 teaspoon beef bouillon powder

In the rest of the bag, combine:
1 tablespoon plus 2 teaspoons dried chopped onion
¼ cup plus 1 tablespoon instant hash browns
2½ tablespoons thinly sliced dried mushrooms
2½ tablespoons dried shredded cabbage
2½ tablespoons thinly sliced dried carrots
¼ teaspoon basil
¼ teaspoon dill
⅛ teaspoon ground caraway or caraway seeds

Pack separately:
2½ tablespoons cream cheese
1 hard-boiled egg (optional)

Phil's Ultra Lite Potatoes with Gravy*

Phil Somers' Ultra Lite Potatoes with Gravy is another variation on the instant potato-meat-vegetable-gravy theme. Phil's is even easier because it uses only one pot. He says it's great on those extra-tough days.

On trail, combine all ingredients and add:
   3 cups boiling water
or more as needed. Stir well and let stand for 10 minutes or until ingredients are fully reconstituted.

Servings: Makes one serving of a little more than 3 cups.
Nutritional information: About 513 calories, 5 grams fat, 87 grams carbohydrate, and 9 grams protein.

At home, pack:
1 ounce freeze-dried beef
1 ounce freeze-dried green beans
1⅓ cups potato flakes
1 envelope gravy mix

Sanna's Mashed Potato Dinner

Says Sanna McKim: "Winter is not the time to think low-fat. You need those fat calories to stay warm long-term." Here's a quick and filling recipe for a winter evening. With pepperoni, scallions, and cheese, you don't really need any seasonings, but garlic, black pepper, or red pepper flakes add extra flavor.

To substitute dried for fresh ingredients, use ½ tablespoon butter powder, 1½ to 2 tablespoons dried green peppers, and ¼ cup thinly sliced dried carrots. Rehydrate vegetables in an insulated container with about ½ cup boiling water for 10 minutes, then drain off water. Add butter powder and combine with reconstituted potatoes.

At home, pack (though not in the same bag):

1½ cups instant mashed potatoes
1 tablespoon butter
3 to 4 scallions or ¼ green pepper
1 small carrot
1 ounce (one 1-inch cube) cheddar cheese
1⅓ inch pepperoni (about 1 ounce)

On trail, add to instant mashed potatoes:

1½ cups boiling water

and let stand 10 minutes. Slice fresh vegetables, cheese, and pepperoni. Fold into mashed potatoes with butter.

Servings: Makes one serving of about 2¼ cups.
Nutritional information: 645 calories, 28 grams fat, 83 grams carbohydrate, and 21 grams protein.

▲ ▲ ▲

Sanna's Trail Tips

"To avoid unnecessary clean-up, forget using a cutting surface. Take the carrot and pepperoni and carefully cut them lengthwise several times a few inches down so that when you slice across as you normally would, each slice produces several diced pieces as you slice over a bowl."

Sanna has her own version of an insulated bowl: "Tuck the bowl into your sleeping bag, with lid tightly secured, as you wait for your companions to finish slaving over their meals. Pull out a book or lean back and enjoy the stars."

Jeff Rennicke's Hot Tips

Jeff is *BACKPACKER*'s Midwest field editor. His latest book, written with a coauthor, is *Exploring Canada's Spectacular National Parks.*

Style: I am a middle-of-the-trail kind of outdoor cook—not known to carry in legs of lamb for basting but also not one to cut my seasoning packets in half to save weight. I strive for balance in all things. I like things light enough not to drag me down on the trail but am willing to carry things that will pick me up at camp. I believe that you can hardly carry too many spices. They are light, easy to pack, and can bring life to even the most dead-on-arrival freeze-dried meals.

Standbys: I am a get-up-and-go-early kind of hiker. I like to get up, snap on the stove under the coffee pot (all set up and ready to light the night before if I am not in bear country), take down the tent and pack, then have coffee and a quick bite to eat before I hit the trail. I hate to do dishes in the morning so anything that requires more than just the quick wipe of a bowl is usually not on the menu. Since I like to be on the trail early (best light, coolest temps, best wildlife sightings possible, fewest people), I will often stop mid-morning for another more leisurely snack (gorp, fruit) to tide me over until lunch.

For lunch, I usually take tortillas because they don't get smashed in your pack, they seem to last longer than bagels or bread, and they can be used for so many things. I also take beef jerky to nibble on as I hike.

Dinner is when the pots and pans come out. I try to get into camp early enough to have light to play with. But I also try to time it so that I am *not* slaving away cooking while the sunset is at its best. I hate missing a good sunset because I have to stir the rice. So, I cook early enough so that I can dine with the sunset or set everything up but don't cook until after the sun is down.

Rice and noodles are my favorite dishes, always using my own spices (the pre-packaged stuff is so salt-heavy). Then, when I can I add fresh vegetables, which add crunch and taste. Fresh green beans last for days and carrots last forever at most temperatures. This is where you get rewarded for carrying something in. I always have something crunchy at dinner. The textures of rice and noodle dishes can get monotonous after a while so something like oyster crackers, fresh carrots, even dry bread sticks can make a meal much more satisfying. Always a dessert—pudding is easy, Mint Milano cookies from the store are magic. Life is good.

MAINLY BEANS AND LENTILS • • • • • • • • • • • • • • • • •

Many outdoorspeople avoid beans and lentils because these legumes require a long cooking time. But with the advent of freeze-dried whole beans, dehydrated flakes, and dehydrated spreads, legumes are no longer the fuel hogs that they once were. Also, if you are willing to carry lentils while they rehydrate, you can cut cooking time markedly.

Note: If you are using plain old beans or lentils from the bag, check carefully for tiny rocks that may have crept through the manufacturing process along with the legumes. What you don't need in the backcountry is a broken tooth.

Also note: If you find that legumes create unacceptable amounts of gas, try one of the "degassing" additives like Beano that are available at the supermarket.

Kristin's Backcountry Burritos

When Kristin Hostetter takes *BACKPACKER* testers into the field, she likes to feed them well to avoid mutiny. "After all, gear testing is not exactly a walk in the park, so a good meal makes up for a lot of aches, pains, and blisters," she says. This meal packs in a lot of carbos to refuel weary hikers. It combines lightweight dried ingredients with a few key fresh ingredients to add fire to the meal. Kristin says that anything goes for the veggies—she usually uses onions, tomatoes, peppers, carrots, and zucchini.

At home, combine:
2 cups lentils
½ cup mixed dried veggies

Pack separately in your spice kit:
2 to 3 cloves garlic
cayenne pepper
Tabasco
½ fresh jalapeño (one if
    you dare)

Also pack:
6 flour tortillas (7½-inch
    diameter)
1 bag of "boil in the bag"
    brown rice (makes 2 cups)

On trail, at lunch time, put the lentils and veggies into a quart-sized, wide-mouthed plastic bottle, cover with water, and let soak all afternoon. Once you're in camp, bring the lentil-veggie mixture to a boil. Add minced garlic, chopped jalapeño, Tabasco, and cayenne pepper, then simmer—covered—until the lentils are tender, about 5 to 10 minutes. Set aside mix and cook the rice per package directions. Use the inverted lids of both cookpots as tortilla warmers. When the rice is done, mix thoroughly with the lentil-veggie mixture and spoon onto warm tortillas. Pass around the bottle of Tabasco for the heat-lovers.

Servings: Makes three servings of 2 burritos each.
Nutritional information: 956 calories, 11 grams fat, 93 grams carbohydrate, and 15 grams protein.

Variation: No-cook Burritos*

Pack 2 cups freeze-dried lentils and 1 cup freeze-dried brown rice or instant rice with the veggie mixture. Bring to a boil:

    4 cups water

Add the lentils, rice, veggies, and seasonings. Mix well, cover, remove from heat, and let stand 10 minutes. Add cayenne and Tabasco to taste.

Servings: Makes three servings of 2 burritos each.
Nutritional information: 749 calories, 12 grams fat, 135 grams carbohydrate, and 28 grams protein.

Red Lentils and Rice

This recipe is not instant, though it doesn't take long to prepare because red lentils cook in about 15 minutes. You can generally find red lentils in large supermarkets but if not, try the health food store. These lentils do tend to turn mushy if overcooked, but not to worry—the basmati rice gives this dish texture.

    Garam masala is an Indian spice blend containing peppercorns, coriander seed, cumin seed, cloves, cardamom seeds, and cinnamon sticks that have been roasted and ground. If you are partial to Indian cooking, you may want to make your own (a good Indian cuisine book should have a recipe), but for general purposes it is easier to buy. Check the spice shelf of your supermarket or health food store.

    If you would like to make this recipe larger, increase the rice by ¼ cup and the water by ½ cup to get an additional ½ cup cooked rice.

At home, combine:
¾ cup red lentils
½ teaspoon ground tumeric
½ teaspoon ground ginger
½ teaspoon salt
¼ teaspoon garam masala
½ teaspoon ground cumin
¼ teaspoon cayenne pepper
½ teaspoon garlic powder
2 tablespoons dried onion
2 tablespoons tomato bits or flakes, or 6 small pieces of dried tomato, quartered
½ cup basmati rice

On trail, bring to a boil:

    3 cups water

and add dry ingredients. Return to a boil and then simmer, stirring occasionally and adding water as needed, so lentils won't stick, for about 15 minutes or until lentils and rice are both done.

Servings: Makes 3 cups or two servings of 1½ cups each.
Nutritional information: 430 calories, 2 grams fat, 80 grams carbohydrate, and 20 grams protein per 1½ cups.

■

At home, combine:
¼ cup freeze-dried white
  beans
¼ cup freeze-dried black
  beans
¼ cup freeze-dried kidney
  beans
¼ cup instant rice
1 tablespoon thinly sliced
  dried carrots
1 tablespoon dried red bell
  pepper, or tomato bits or
  flakes
1 tablespoon dried onion
½ teaspoon garlic powder
1 teaspoon ground cumin
  (or to taste)
1 teaspoon chili powder
  (or to taste)
1 teaspoon cilantro or parsley
1 teaspoon potato starch
  (optional)

■

At home, pack:
1 tablespoon tomato bits or
  flakes
1 tablespoon dried bell
  pepper
1½ teaspoons dried onion
3 tablespoons freeze-dried
  corn
½ cup dried refried beans
salsa leather equivalent to
  2 tablespoons salsa (or
  more to taste)

Also pack:
1 corn or flour tortilla
1 ounce (one 1-inch cube)
  cheddar cheese

Three-Bean Stew*

The varied colors in this dish—white, black, red, green, and orange—give it great presentation appeal, which means that it looks good and invites you to dig right in. While it's true that with a short cooking time, the flavors of the cumin and chili do not develop as they would if they had simmered, the ingredients as a whole provide lots of flavor. Of course you can make this stew with one type of bean, but you'll lose some of the variety in texture and visual appeal.

Possible acompaniments include: ½ to 1 ounce diced cheddar cheese, a few tablespoons of salsa, ¼ cup crushed corn chips, and hot sauce to taste.

On trail, place dry ingredients in an insulated bowl, add:
  1 cup boiling water
(or more, if you like a stew with lots of liquid), cover, and let stand 10 minutes. Add salt to taste.

Servings: Makes one serving of about 1½ cups.
Nutritional information: 309 calories, 1 gram fat, 62 grams carbohydrate, and 14 grams protein; with 1 ounce cheese, 379 calories, 5 grams fat, 62 grams carbohydrate, and 20 grams protein.

Tamale Pie Freestyle*

A tamale is cornmeal dough with a meat and chile filling that is wrapped in a corn husk and steamed. Tamale Pie is a spinoff that combines a cornbread crust with a chile or bean topping. This tamale recipe goes freestyle—no crust—so that it can be prepared with just the addition of boiling water. Instant refried beans are handy for this recipe.

On trail, place dry ingredients in an insulated bowl and add:
  1 cup plus 2 tablespoons boiling water
Stir, cover, and let stand for 10 minutes. Meanwhile, dice the cheese and tear half the tortilla into small pieces. When the veggie-bean mix has rehydrated, stir in the cheese and tortilla pieces. Add salt, pepper, and hot sauce to taste. Eat with the remainder of the tortilla.

Servings: Makes one serving of about 1¾ cups.
Nutritional information: 460 calories, 9 grams fat, 86 grams carbohydrate, and 29 grams protein.

RICE •

The recipes in this section represent a widespread sampling of flavors from curry to turkey, from Creole to sushi. Instant "one-minute" brown or white rice or freeze-dried brown rice all work in the following no-cook recipes, so you can take your pick.

Curried Rice and Chickpeas*

This recipe uses a product right off the supermarket shelf—dehydrated hummus—to make an intriguing dinner. The olive oil adds subtle flavor and calories and though the lemon juice is not critical, it is nice. A couple of single-serving portions of lemon juice can fill the bill.

On trail, place the rice-veggie mixture in an insulated bowl and add:
   ¾ cup minus 1 tablespoon boiling water
Mix well, cover, and let stand 10 minutes. Then, add the dried hummus and seasonings, lemon juice, and olive oil. Stir well, re-cover, and let stand for 3 minutes. Add salt or soy sauce to taste.

Servings: Makes one serving of about 1½ cups.
Nutritional information: Including optional olive oil, 379 calories, 7 grams fat, 64 grams carbohydrate, and 14 grams protein.

How to make tomato powder

If you don't have tomato powder on hand, toss tomato bits or flakes into the blender and blend away. One-fourth cup tomato bits makes a little more than 3 tablespoons and ¼ cup tomato flakes makes about 2 tablespoons tomato powder.

■

At home, combine in a plastic bag:
¼ cup plus 2 tablespoons instant rice
2 tablespoons tomato bits or flakes
3 tablespoons dried cabbage
2 teaspoons dried onion
¼ teaspoon garlic powder

In another bag, pack:
3 tablespoons dried hummus
2 teaspoons tomato powder
⅓ teaspoon curry powder
1 teaspoon coconut cream powder or powdered coconut

If desired, pack along:
soy sauce
2 small packets of lemon juice (optional)
1 teaspoon or so olive oil (optional)

Rice with Turkey and Cranberries*

Follow this entrée with a dessert of mincemeat pudding and you have an easy theme dinner. If you are doubling the recipe for yourself or sharing with your hiking partner, substitute a small can of turkey for the freeze-dried turkey called for here. Wild rice is exellent in this dish. If you use wild rice that has been cooked and dried (rather than the freeze-dried rice called for in the recipe), simmer all ingredients per package instructions, adding water as needed.

■

At home, combine:
½ cup instant white rice or freeze-dried wild rice
2 tablespoons thinly sliced dried mushrooms
2 tablespoons freeze-dried turkey
1 tablespoon plus 1 teaspoon dried cranberries
1 teaspoon dried onions
¼ teaspoon garlic powder
½ teaspoon chicken bouillon powder
½ teaspoon parsley

On trail, place dry ingredients in an insulated bowl and add:
1¼ cups boiling water.
Stir well, cover, and let stand 10 minutes.

Servings: Makes one serving of about 1½ cups.
Nutritional information: 342 calories, 4 grams fat, 71 grams carbohydrate, and 8 grams protein.

Shrimp Creole*

This recipe combines shrimp, rice, tomatoes, peppers, and spicy seasoning in a recipe reminiscent of the bayous of the Louisiana coast. The recipe is set up for one person—and a whole can of shrimp—but you can stretch a can if you double the recipe. Because some brands of dried celery take longer than 10 minutes to rehydrate, test yours at home to make sure you'll be satisfied on trail.

■

At home, combine:
⅓ cup instant rice
2 tablespoons tomato bits or flakes, or dried tomatoes cut in pieces
1 tablespoon plus 1 teaspoon tomato powder
1 tablespoon dried onion
2 teaspoons dried pepper
2 teaspoons dried celery
1 teaspoon potato starch
½ teaspoon dried parsley
⅛ teaspoon garlic powder
⅛ teaspoon sugar

Also pack:
1 (4-ounce) can shrimp

On trail, place dry ingredients in an insulated bowl and add:
1 cup boiling water
Cover and let stand 10 minutes. Add drained shrimp, then season with:
½ to 1 teaspoon Worcestershire sauce or to taste
dash Tabasco to taste
salt and pepper to taste

Servings: Using a whole can of shrimp, makes one serving of about 1¾ cups; using ½ can shrimp, makes one serving of about 1½ cups.
Nutritional information: Using a whole can of shrimp, 285 calories, trace fat, 14 grams carbohydrate, and 21 grams protein.

▲ ▲ ▲

Thanksgiving in July

For a special evening on an extra-special trip, I served up a truly sumptuous meal. For an appetizer I reconstituted sweet pumpkin soup (made the winter before, dried, and powdered in the blender). As an entrée we had wild rice with broccoli, zucchini, and red bell peppers (all vegetables rehydrated) accompanied by sweet potatoes (also rehydrated) and cranberry-orange relish (see page 71). For dessert we dug into mincemeat pudding (see page 139). It was, indeed, a day of Thanksgiving.

Sanna's Scrambled Sushi Dinner*

Sanna McKim recommends this dish as a desert food. Salt in the nori (a seaweed that comes in flat sheets) and soy sauce replaces the salt you've sweated out and zingy flavors in the wasabi (a very strong horseradish powder) and ginger keep your taste buds jumping. You can buy dried tofu at a health food store or make your own (see page 101). Look for nori, pickled ginger, and wasabi in an Asian market or a health food store if you cannot find them in your local supermarket. If you have not had wasabi before, mix up a little and taste it at home to make sure that it agrees with you. In the event that you are planning a meal for a group, omit the wasabi from the recipe and carry it separately in your spice kit.

On trail, slice the carrot, if using fresh. Otherwise place dry ingredients in an insulated bowl and add:

    2 cups boiling water (2½ cups if using dried carrots)

Stir, cover, and let stand 10 minutes or until the tofu has rehydrated. Season with pickled ginger and soy sauce to taste.

Servings: Makes one serving of about 2 cups.
Nutritional information: About 411 calories, 6 grams fat, 72 grams carbohydrate, and 16 grams protein.

At home, combine:
¾ cup instant rice
2 sheets nori, broken into
    pieces
dash wasabi
1 square commercially dried
    tofu or several slices
    home-dried tofu
1 small carrot or ¼ cup
    thinly sliced dried carrots

Pack in separate containers:
3 slices pickled ginger
soy sauce to taste

WRAPS •

A burrito is hand-held food made of a soft tortilla that has been warmed and filled, then folded so the filling stays inside. A wrap is the same idea, only you can use any thin, flat bread. Some food emporiums make their own flavored flatbreads, with spinach and other yummy ingredients. But supermarkets may carry only one or two kinds of flatbread, including tortillas, so I've called for tortillas here.

If the weather is wretched and you don't feel like rolling wraps, rehydrate the filling and eat it as a stew with the flatbread as a side dish. (As much fun as wraps are, they do require that extra step.) If I know ahead that I won't be wrapping, I include 2 to 4 extra table-spoons of carbohydrate to bulk up the dish, and then add a few extra tablespoons of boiling water to rehydrate the carbo.

Beef-Vegetable Wraps*

At home, pack:

3 tablespoons dried ground beef

¼ cup plus 2 tablespoons instant hash browns

¼ cup thinly sliced dried carrots

¼ cup thinly sliced dried tomatoes

1 tablespoon dried onions

Pack separately:

salsa leather equivalent to ½ cup salsa

4 tortillas (7½-inch diameter)

On trail, put dry meat-veggie mix in insulated bowl and add:

1 cup plus 3 tablespoons boiling water

Mix well, cover, and let stand for 10 minutes. Meanwhile, reconstitute the salsa leather separately by adding:

½ cup boiling water

Cover and let stand 10 minutes or until the salsa has rehydrated. Briefly heat tortillas in frying pan or pot lid. When both parts of the wrap have rehydrated, drain the water (if there is any) from the meat and veggies, then add the reconstituted salsa. Add salt and pepper to taste. Spoon ½ cup filling onto each tortilla, turn in sides, and roll.

Servings: Makes 2 cups filling, enough for 4 wraps.
Nutritional information: 394 calories, 18 grams fat, 137 grams carbohydrate, and 22 grams protein per recipe.

Variation: Beef Vegetable Wraps With Gravy*

At home, omit the salsa and pack separately:

½ package of gravy mix (1 cup size)

On trail, reconstitute meat-veggie mixture as above only increase the water to a total of:

1½ cups boiling water

After the filling has rehydrated for 10 minutes, add the gravy mix and let stand for 2 more minutes.

Nutritional information: 794 calories, 19 grams fat, 135 grams carbohydrate, and 22 grams protein per recipe.

Variation: Beef Vegetable Wraps With Herbs and Cheese*

Instead of salsa or gravy, season with cheese and various herbs.

At home, place the following ingredients in a plastic bag and tie off:

1½ teaspoons basil, oregano, and other green herbs of choice

1 teaspoon butter powder

½ teaspoon garlic powder

1½ tablespoons cheese powder

Then, add the meat and vegetables to the bag.

On trail, rehydrate the meat and vegetables according to previous recipe, then add seasonings.

Nutritional information: 827 calories, 23 grams fat, 132 grams carbohydrate, and 24 grams protein per recipe.

▲ ▲ ▲

How to Roll Wraps

Lay a tortilla or piece of flatbread on a flat surface. Place ½ cup of filling in the center of the tortilla, as shown, stopping short of the edges. Turn the side edges in toward the filling. Fold the near edge away from you and tuck it under the filling. Bring the far edge toward you in a tight roll. If the wrap is properly made, the filling should stay inside.

Beef and Cabbage Wraps*

The deep, roasted flavor of the nuts complements the rehydrated ground beef, and together they make for a real-food texture that's always welcome on trail.

For a wrap with even more gusto, omit the garlic and cayenne pepper and add wasabi (powdered horseradish). One-half teaspoon provides a hint (but not an overwhelming amount) of flavor. Increase the wasabi to taste, but taste as you go—it's potent stuff!

On trail, place dry ingredients in an insulated bowl and add:
    1 cup boiling water
Stir well, cover, and let stand 10 minutes. Meanwhile, briefly heat tortillas in frying pan or pot lid. When the filling has rehydrated, add salt or soy sauce to taste. Spoon ½ cup filling onto each tortilla, turn in the sides, and roll.

Servings: Makes 2 cups filling, enough for 4 wraps.
Nutritional information: 859 calories, 29 grams fat, 131 grams carbohydrate, and 27 grams protein per recipe.

■
At home, combine:
¼ **cup dried ground beef**
¼ **cup plus 2 tablespoons dried cabbage**
¼ **cup instant rice**
2 tablespoons toasted pine nuts or walnuts
½ **teaspoon onion**
½ **teaspoon parsley**
½ **teaspoon dill**
⅛ **teaspoon garlic powder (or to taste)**
few grains cayenne pepper (or to taste)
Also pack:
4 tortillas (7½-inch diameter)

Turkey Tagine Wraps*

A tagine is a Moroccan stew made with fish, poultry, or meat and vegetables or fruit, all of which is cooked in a traditional covered earthenware dish. This recipe is adapted from turkey tagine, though a no-cook wrap is pretty distant from a long-simmered stew.

Dried ginger rehydrates so it's as good as fresh, but if you want the real thing (and fresh ginger does carry well on trail), then pack some along. If you are using fresh ginger, mince it and add it just before you make this dish. If your kitchen is stocked with ground ginger rather than dried or fresh ginger, place ½ teaspoon ground ginger in the corner of a plastic bag, tie it off, then add the other dry ingredients. On trail, add the powder after you've drained off the excess water.

The olives are not essential, but they add an exotic flavor, and they should keep well enough for the first few days of a trip.

On trail, place dry ingredients and turkey in an insulated bowl and add:

1 cup boiling water

Stir, cover, and let stand 10 minutes. Meanwhile, briefly heat tortillas in a frying pan or pot lid. When filling has rehydrated, drain broth and add salt to taste; add turkey. Stir in sliced green olives if you are using them. Spoon ½ cup filling onto each tortilla, turn in the sides, and roll.

Servings: Makes 2 cups filling, enough for 4 wraps.
Nutritional information: 1194 calories, 50 grams fat, 129 grams carbohydrate, and 55 grams protein per recipe.

At home, combine:
¼ cup instant rice
¼ cup toasted almonds
2 tablespoons dried onion
2 teaspoons cilantro
1 teaspoon minced dried ginger
½ teaspoon dried lemon rind

Pack separately (optional):
8 green olives

Also pack:
4 tortillas (7½-inch diameter)
1 (5-ounce) can turkey

Cashew Chicken Wraps*

In this recipe, it is important to use pineapple and coconut without added sugar. If you can't find unsweetened versions in your supermarket, try your local health food store. Also, you can substitute coconut cream powder for coconut flakes by adding 1½ teaspoons powder to the cashews rather than the cabbage mixture.

■

At home, place in a plastic bag and tie off:
¾ cup toasted cashews

Then add to bag:
¼ cup plus 2 tablespoons dried cabbage
¼ cup plus 2 tablespoons thinly sliced dried mushrooms
2 tablespoons dried pineapple (optional)
1 tablespoon dried onion
1 tablespoon flaked coconut

Pack separately:
1 (5-ounce) can chicken
4 tortillas (7 ½-inch diameter)

On trail, place cabbage mixture in an insulated bowl and add:
¾ cup boiling water

Stir well, cover, and let stand 10 minutes. Meanwhile, briefly heat tortillas in frying pan or pot lid. When the filling has rehydrated, drain excess water. Add cashews, chicken, and salt to taste. Spoon ½ cup filling onto each tortilla, turn in the sides, and roll.

Servings: Makes about 2 cups filling, enough for 4 wraps.
Nutritional information: 1171 calories, 31 grams fat, 142 grams carbohydrate, and 74 grams protein per recipe.

Buck O'Herin's Hot Tips

Buck is owner and chief guide for Earth Treks in Montville, Maine. Like other guides, he knows that food can make or break a trip, so it's important to make the extra effort to provide good food.

Style: Gourmand

Standbys: If oatmeal or muesli are garnished with nuts, raisins, cinnamon, nutmeg, butter, and/or maple syrup, people start to look forward to breakfast. (Also see page 112 for Buck's Couscous with Feta Cheese.)

Favorite gadget: A dehydrator

Trail wisdom: I find that with a little extra effort and creativity food cravings, which sometimes feel like a pack of hungry dogs, can be held at bay.

Thai Shrimp Wraps*

This wrap has a light but surprisingly tasty flavor. See the Turkey Tagine recipe for tips on substituting fresh or ground ginger for dried ginger.

On trail, place dry ingredients in an insulated bowl and add:
> 3 tablespoons boiling water

Mix well, cover, and let stand 10 minutes. Meanwhile, briefly heat tortillas in frying pan or pot lid. Add drained shrimp to filling. Spoon ½ cup filling onto each tortilla, turn in the sides, and roll.

Servings: Makes about 2 cups filling, enough for 4 wraps.
Nutritional information: 1027 calories, 30 grams fat, 150 grams carbohydrate, and 41 grams protein per recipe.

At home, combine:
½ cup instant rice
1 tablespoon plus 1 teaspoon dried onion
1 tablespoon plus 1 teaspoon coconut cream powder or powdered coconut
1 tablespoon plus 1 teaspoon cilantro
1 teaspoon minced dried ginger
⅛ teaspoon garlic powder

Pack separately:
1 (5-ounce) can shrimp
4 tortillas (7½-inch diameter)

Szechuan Veggie Wraps*

The cashews and rehydrated cabbage in this recipe give the filling a nice crunchy texture, while the peanut butter, bouillon, and other seasonings give it taste.

On trail, place mushroom mix in an insulated bowl and add:
> 1¼ cups boiling water

Stir well, cover, and let stand 10 minutes. Meanwhile, briefly heat tortillas in frying pan or pot lid. When veggies have rehydrated, stir in peanut butter mixture and salt or soy sauce to taste. Spoon ½ cup filling onto each tortilla, turn in sides, and roll.

Servings: Makes about 2 cups filling, enough for 4 wraps.
Nutritional information: 1315 calories, 37 grams fat, 157 grams carbohydrate, 62 grams protein per recipe.

At home, combine and mix well in a plastic bag:
½ cup toasted chopped cashews
2 tablespoons peanut butter
1 teaspoon bouillon powder
1 tablespoon powdered milk

Tie off above ingredients, then add:
½ cup thinly sliced dried mushrooms
½ cup dried cabbage
1 tablespoon plus 1 teaspoon dried onion
1 teaspoon ground ginger
⅛ teaspoon garlic powder

Also pack:
4 tortillas (7½-inch) diameter

OTHER DINNERS • • • • • • • • • • • • • •

This last section of entrées includes two trail favorites, pizza and stuffing.

Pizza

If you have a baking device, plenty of fuel, and patience, you can fulfill what many folks consider their biggest food fantasy: backcountry pizza. This isn't a sort-of pizza but a full-fledged, yeast-dough pizza with the kind of toppings you would find in a good pizzeria. Sun-dried tomatoes, rehydrated mushrooms, and pepperoni are favorites, or, you can experiment with anything from broccoli to asparagus. (To make spaghetti leather for the sauce, see pages 33–34.)

For extra pizazz in the crust, add a tablespoon or two of grated Parmesan cheese, tomato powder, or spinach powder to the crust ingredients. To make a crust from nirvana, substitute ¼ cup bread base—such as spinach and feta bread base, black olive bread base, or any other pepped up flour that catches your fancy—for ¼ cup of the whole wheat flour.

At home, for the crust, mix well and place in a plastic bag:
¾ **cup unbleached white flour**
¾ **cup whole wheat flour**
½ **teaspoon salt**
2 **teaspoons yeast**
2 **tablespoons oil**

For the sauce, in another bag place:
spaghetti leather equivalent to ½ cup sauce (more to taste)

In a third bag place ½ cup dried veggies (your choice) perhaps including:
¼ **cup thinly sliced dried tomatoes**
¼ **cup thinly sliced dried mushrooms**

Also pack:
one or two 1-ounce sticks of string (mozzarella) cheese

On trail, add to veggies:
1 **cup boiling water**
Tomatoes and mushrooms should rehydrate fully in about 10 minutes; freeze-dried veggies will take less time. Rehydrate spaghetti leather separately by adding:
½ **cup boiling water**
For crust, reserve 2 to 3 tablespoons flour mixture, then add ½ cup warm water to crust ingredients. Water should be warm to the touch, but not hot. If you add hot water you may kill the yeast and if you add cool water the yeast will not activate; either way, you'll have flatbread instead of risen bread.

Mix dough with a spoon, then knead for about 5 minutes, using reserved flour mixture as necessary. Let dough stand for 10 minutes, then flatten it in a greased pan or, if using a boil-in-a-bag baking device, in an oven bag, bringing the edges up about ½ inch. Add sauce/veggie mixture. Top with mozzarella cheese. (If using a boil-in-a-bag type baker, reserve cheese and add after pizza is baked so that cheese won't stick to the bag.)

For a *backpacking Dutch oven (7½ inches in diameter)*, bake 20 to 25 minutes or until done.

For a *boil-in-a-bag type baker (5½ inches in diameter)*, using half the recipe, bake/boil in a small oven bag 12 to 14 minutes and let stand 3 minutes.

For a *boil-in-a-bag type baker (7½ inches in diameter)*, bake/boil in a medium or large oven bag 15 minutes and let stand 5 minutes.

For a *convection-oven type baker (6 to 7½ inches in diameter)*, bake 20 to 25 minutes or until done.

Servings: Makes one 6- to 8-inch pizza.
Nutritional information: Using 2 ounces string cheese, 1192 calories, 55 grams fat, 158 grams carbohydrate, and 34 grams protein per recipe.

▲ ▲ ▲

Making Yeast Dough on a Cool Day

If it is a cool, cloudy day and you think the yeast may not activate enough to make the bread rise, place the kneaded dough in a plastic bag that has room for expansion and position it inside your shirt against your warm body. Or, place the plastic bag—making sure there are no holes—in a pot of water that is barely warm to the touch but no hotter. Let the dough rest 10 minutes or longer until you can see that it has risen somewhat and therefore know that the yeast is alive.

If you are unsure of your baking skills, add 1½ teaspoons baking powder to the dry ingredients. Even if the yeast fails, the dough will rise when it bakes.

Variation: Pesto Pizza

Pesto should not be left unrefrigerated longer than 36 hours (it could develop the botulinus toxin), so use fresh the first night only.

On trail, make pizza crust and rehydrate veggies as above. When crust is ready, spread the pesto over the crust, then put on the rehydrated veggies. Sprinkle with Parmesan cheese and bake as above.

Nutritional information: 1277 calories, 65 grams fat, 155 grams carbohydrate, and 34 grams protein per recipe.

At home, follow the above recipe, except omit the spaghetti leather and string cheese and pack:
¼ **cup pesto**
¼ **cup Parmesan cheese**
or:
½ **envelope pesto sauce**
5 **tablespoons Parmesean cheese**

plus (pack separately):
1 **tablespoon olive oil**

Cornbread Stuffing

This dish builds on the long tradition among backpackers of combining commercial stuffing mix and instant gravy mix to make a filling hot meal. The veggies add fresh flavor and the cornbread stuffing—rather than regular stuffing—provides a new twist.

If you substitute instant gravy mix for the bouillon and potato starch called for below, use the amount needed to make ¼ cup gravy (about 1 tablespoon). In either case, it is quicker to reconstitute the veggies in plain water than with the gravy ingredients; if you pack the veggies and gravy together, cook them a few minutes extra and add a little extra water as needed.

■

At home, combine in a plastic bag and tie off:

1 teaspoon bouillon powder
1 teaspoon potato starch

In the rest of the bag, pack:

1 tablespoon dried onion
3 tablespoons thinly sliced dried carrots
2 tablespoons thinly sliced dried mushrooms
⅛ teaspoon garlic powder
1 teaspoon parsley
¼ teaspoon thyme
pinch marjoram
pinch sage

Pack separately:

2 tablespoons chopped walnuts
1 cup cornbread stuffing

On trail, place veggie mixture in a pot and add:

1 cup water

and bring water to a boil. Simmer for several minutes until the veggies have rehydrated. Add the gravy ingredients and stir until the gravy thickens. Add the stuffing and walnuts.

Servings: Makes one serving of a little more than 1½ cups.
Nutritional information: 369 calories, 13 grams fat, 57 grams carbohydrate, 9 grams protein.

▲ ▲ ▲

Store-bought Stuffing with Lots of Stuff

No longer is store-bought stuffing limited to bread cubes and herbs. If your at-home prep time is short, check out the more elaborate stuffing mixes—one variety I found contains wild rice, mushrooms, onions, red bell peppers, and tomatoes. Fold in some chicken or turkey, and you have an easy meal.

Variation: Cornbread Stuffing with Chicken

Add a 5-ounce can chicken or ⅔ cup rehydrated freeze-dried chicken when you add the stuffing.

Nutritional information: 519 calories, 16 grams fat, 57 grams carbohydrate, and 39 grams protein.

CHAPTER 7

Desserts

While eating supper we very naturally speak of better fare, as musty bread and spoiled bacon are not palatable. Soon I see Hawkins down by the boat, taking up the sextant—rather a strange proceeding for him—and I question him concerning it. He replies that he is trying to find the latitude and longitude of the nearest pie.

John Wesley Powell,
The Exploration of the Colorado River and its Canyons, 1895

For those with a sweet tooth, desserts are not merely an appendage to dinner, they are the highlight of the meal. A cup of hot cocoa and a few fig bars may suffice, but if you are willing to devote a few minutes to the task, you can whip up one of a wide selection of puddings, cakes, and pies . . . and you won't even need a sextant to find them.

PUDDINGS • • • • • • • • • • • • • • • • • •

Commercial instant puddings, which can be paired with various dried fruits, couldn't be easier—add cold water and wait. The made-from-scratch instant puddings that follow aren't much harder, and they offer some wonderful variations.

John's Dessert to Die For*

These desserts are some of John Emelin's favorites. They are very simple—it's the pudding and fruit combination that gives the great taste. Use store-bought instant pudding and dehydrated fruit (or, if your store doesn't sell the fruit mentioned, dehydrate your own). John says his best combos are vanilla pudding with strawberries, chocolate pudding with raspberries, banana pudding with bananas or strawberries, and "the real surprise," butterscotch pudding with kiwi fruit.

Coconut-Mango Rice Pudding*

The coconut here goes nicely with the mango in this variation on rice pudding. You can, of course, substitute other types of dried fruit; apricots are a good choice.

■

At home, place in a plastic bag and mix well:

½ teaspoon potato starch
2 tablespoons powdered milk
1½ teaspoons coconut cream powder or powdered coconut
½ teaspoon sugar

Then add:
1 tablespoon chopped dried mango
½ cup instant rice

On trail, place ingredients in an insulated mug and add:
    ½ cup boiling water
Stir well, cover, and let stand 5 minutes.

Servings: Makes one serving of a little more than ½ cup.
Nutritional information: 304 calories, 8 grams fat, 56 grams carbohydrate, and 5 grams protein.

▲ ▲ ▲
Using Potato Starch
When using potato starch, make sure it is evenly dispersed in the dry mix. Otherwise, it will form lumps when you add water.

Coconut Cream Pudding*

I wasn't sure whether to call this a dessert or a beverage—it's thicker than milk but not as thick as pudding. The fat in the coconut makes this dish tasty and satisfying.

For a variation, add ½ teaspoon ground ginger.

On trail, place ingredients in an insulated mug and add:
   1 cup boiling water
Stir well, cover, and let stand 5 minutes.

Servings: Makes one serving of 1 cup or two servings of ½ cup each.
Nutritional information: 258 calories, 10 grams fat, 38 grams carbohydrate, and 4 grams protein per recipe.

■

At home, combine:
1 tablespoon plus 1 teaspoon sugar
¼ cup powdered milk
1 tablespoon plus 1 teaspoon potato starch
1 tablespoon coconut cream powder or powdered coconut

Mincemeat Pudding*

Planning a Thanksgiving or Christmas trip? Mincemeat Pudding is quick, easy, and oh-so-tasty. You can almost hear the sleigh bells ringing.

On trail, crumble mincemeat into an insulated cup or bowl. Add:
   ½ cup boiling water
Cover and let stand for 10 minutes. Sprinkle the crumbled graham cracker on top.

Servings: Makes one serving of a little more than ¾ cup.
Nutritional information: 333 calories, 2 grams fat, 77 grams carbohydrate, and 1 gram protein.

©Ben Townsend

Mincemeat pudding in a graham cracker crust makes an impressive special-event dessert.

■

At home, pack in a plastic bag and tie off:
1 crumbled graham cracker (optional)

Then add to the remainder of the bag:
3 ounces (⅓ of a 9-ounce package) condensed mincemeat

Mincemeat without the Meat*

Where's the beef? Not here. This vegetarian recipe provides the same rich flavors, though. The dried apple juice and potato starch are optional but contribute to the texture.

■

At home, combine:
2 tablespoons chopped dates
1 tablespoon raisins
1½ tablespoons chopped dried apple (about 1 ring)
1 tablespoon chopped walnuts
¼ teaspoon candied ginger
1 teaspoon dried cider or apple juice mix (optional)
½ teaspoon potato starch (optional)

Mix well, making sure the dried apple juice and potato starch are well dispersed.

On trail, place ingredients in an insulated bowl or cup and add:
¼ cup boiling water
Stir well, cover, and let stand 10 minutes.

Servings: Makes one serving of ½ cup.
Nutritional information: 193 calories, 5 grams fat, 38 grams carbohydrate, and 2 grams protein.

Sweet Polenta Pudding for Two

Vanilla powder is the secret ingredient in this easy but unusual dessert. Use sugar according to taste; 4 teaspoons is not very sweet and 6 teaspoons is very sweet. If you can't find a quick-cooking polenta without vegetables added, use cornmeal.

■

At home, place in the corner of a plastic bag and tie off:
1 teaspoon vanilla powder

In the rest of the bag, combine:
½ cup powdered milk
¼ cup quick-cooking polenta or cornmeal
4 to 6 teaspoons sugar
2 tablespoons or more diced dried apricots

On trail, place cornmeal mixture in a pot and add:
1⅓ cups water
Bring to a boil and simmer until the pudding turns thick enough to eat with a spoon. Remove from heat, spoon into individual dishes, and sprinkle on the vanilla powder.

Servings: Makes two servings of ⅔ cup each.
Nutritional information: 181 calories, trace grams fat, 39 grams carbohydrate, and 7 grams protein.

STEAMED PUDDINGS • • • • • • • • •

In texture, steamed puddings fall halfway between puddings and cakes. The firm texture with a slight crumb provides a delightful change from the instant gelled or thick puddings presented above. A big plus with these steamed puddings is that you can make them without a trail baker. Just mix the ingredients with water in a small oven bag, place the bag in boiling water, and wait 10 minutes until your dessert is done. There's no clean-up, either.

This method makes one generous serving or two small servings. If there are two of you and you both like big desserts, make individual puddings one after the other. That way, you can choose what you want, rather than eating what your partner is cooking.

▲ ▲ ▲

Directions for Steaming Puddings and Baking Cakes and Muffins

After you've added water to the dry ingredients in an oven bag, mix well so that there are no dry lumps. Tie the bag closed and form the bag into a rough circle that will fit nicely into your pot.

Place the bag in a pot with 1½ inches boiling water, trying to keep the bag on the surface of the water in as horizontal a position as possible. Adjust the stove so that the water is boiling harder than a mild simmer but not as hard as a rolling boil.

Remove from heat at the indicated time, let stand 3 minutes, and then cut open the bag to allow steam to vent.

If you are headed for the high mountains, see High-altitude Baking, page 147.

▲ ▲ ▲

Measuring odd amounts

To get ¹⁄₁₆ teaspoon, measure ⅛ teaspoon and use half. To measure other odd amounts, choose the measuring spoon that's slightly smaller and heap, or choose the measuring spoon that's slightly larger and use a scant amount. To get ⅙ teaspoon, for example, use a heaping ⅛ teaspoon or a scant ¼ teaspoon.

Jean's Bread Pudding

Jean Spangenberg is a connoisseur of bread pudding—her mother made it often, using leftover biscuits (baked daily), and topping it with homemade jam and fluffy browned meringue. Jean's backcountry version, though, is not as complicated. Powdered sugar is now available in chocolate, lemon, and strawberry flavors, so take your pick.

If you don't have stale bread, cake, or muffins handy, substitute bread crumbs.

At home, combine ingredients and mix well in a small oven bag:

¼ cup stale bread, cake, or muffins
2 tablespoons powdered milk
2 teaspoons powdered eggs
2 teaspoons butter powder
¹⁄₁₆ teaspoon vanilla powder
⅙ teaspoon baking powder

In another bag, pack:
1½ teaspoons flavored powdered sugar

Store in refrigerator or freezer.

On trail, add:
2½ tablespoons water

to the bag with the pudding mixture and let stand 10 minutes to soften the bread. Stir to blend well. Tie bag closed and boil for 10 minutes or until set (see directions on previous page). Sprinkle with flavored powdered sugar. Or, fry the pudding like a pancake and sprinkle with sugar before serving.

Servings: Makes one serving of a little more than ¾ cup or two servings of half that amount.

Nutritional information: Using bread crumbs, 412 calories, 13 grams fat, 55 grams carbohydrate, and 18 grams protein per recipe.

Steamed Apple Pudding

The robust flavor of apples, with a hint of lemon in the sauce, makes this dessert worth the time spent assembling ingredients. Look for dried zest in the spice section of your supermarket or health food store, or see below to make your own.

On trail, to bag of pudding add:

¼ cup plus 1 tablespoon water

Mix well and close bag with tie. Cook for 10 minutes per directions on page 141. Meanwhile, add water gradually to bag containing sauce ingredients. Start with ⅓ teaspoon and then add a few drops at a time (it is easy to make the sauce too runny), using about:

⅔ teaspoon water

Pour lemon sauce over pudding.

Servings: Each bag makes one serving of 1 cup or two servings of ½ cup each.

Nutritional information: 441 calories, 6 grams fat, 90 grams carbohydrate, and 8 grams protein per recipe.

At home, combine ingredients and mix well in a small oven bag:

1½ teaspoons butter powder

1 teaspoon powdered eggs

1½ tablespoons brown sugar

⅛ teaspoon dried orange zest (optional)

3 tablespoons flour

1/16 teaspoon baking soda

⅛ teaspoon baking powder

⅛ teaspoon ground ginger

⅛ teaspoon cinnamon

1½ teaspoons buttermilk powder

1 tablespoon chopped dried apple (1 ring)

Pack sauce ingredients in another bag:

½ to 1 tablespoon powdered sugar

generous pinch dried lemon zest

Store in refrigerator or freezer.

▲ ▲ ▲

Making Zest

Zest is the grated rind of oranges, tangerines, lemons, or limes. To make zest, grate the rind on a fine grater, being careful to get just the colored outer coating and not the bitter inner layer. Spread the zest in a thin layer and leave out overnight. The zest should dry easily, but if the humidity is high or you are in a hurry, place the rind in a toaster oven set to "warm" and remove as soon as it is dry.

Steamed Date Pudding

At home, combine ingredients and mix well in a small oven bag:

1 tablespoon plus 1 teaspoon brown sugar
1 teaspoon butter powder
1 teaspoon powdered eggs
1/16 teaspoon vanilla powder
2 tablespoons flour
1/4 teaspoon baking powder
scant 1/16 teaspoon salt
1 1/2 teaspoons powdered milk
1 tablespoon chopped dates
1 tablespoon chopped nuts

Store in refrigerator or freezer.

On trail, add to bag:
   3 tablespoons water
Mix well. Cook 10 minutes per directions on page 141.

Servings: Each bag makes one serving of slightly more than 3/4 cup or two servings of half that amount.
Nutritional information: 501 calories, 13 grams fat, 105 grams carbohydrate, and 8 grams protein per recipe.

Quick Steamed Brownie Pudding

Chocolate-lovers will appreciate one more way to squeeze chocolate into the day. Use a brownie mix that has a ratio of ingredients comparable to the following: 1 1/2 cups brownie mix, 2 eggs, 1/2 cup nuts. For a fudge-like consistency, add an extra tablespoon of water per serving. As a variation, add 2 tablespoons dried cherries.

At home, combine in a small oven bag:

1/2 cup brownie mix
1 tablespoon powdered eggs
2 1/2 tablespoons chopped walnuts

Store in refrigerator or freezer.

On trail, add to bag:
   3 tablespoons water
Mix ingredients well, close bag with tie, and cook according to directions on page 141.

Servings: Each bag makes one serving of 1 cup or two servings of 1/2 cup each.
Nutritional information: 498 calories, 17 grams fat, 65 grams carbohydrate, and 10 grams protein per recipe.

Sanna McKim's Hot Tips

As a student and faculty member of Audubon Expedition Institute, an educational program in Belfast, Maine, that offers college and graduate degrees in Environmental Studies and Environmental Education, Sanna McKim has camped throughout the United States and Canada.

Style: I am most definitely a mixed breed potlicker/gourmand. I demand minimal prep, cooking, and clean-up (especially when water is scarce or when a main concern is staying warm). But I won't settle for anything less than pleasurable, flavorful, and well-balanced meals that are comforting and satisfying.

Trail wisdom: While wandering supermarket aisles on a full stomach, imagine pushing yourself physically and sleeping out in the climate you'll soon be in. Try to visualize which foods will taste good then, not which ones you normally eat or are currently craving. This is more important than it sounds. If you're headed for arctic conditions, warming foods will serve you well. Dry, desert conditions will make you drool for salty or refreshing foods. Keep in mind what's good for your body, since you'll need it to be performing well for you. Try to include a few different-colored fresh fruits and vegetables that are light, will last, aren't too messy, and don't create leftovers (like banana peels) that you have to carry out.

I like one-pot meals that can be made with only a few cups of boiling water and a bowl with a lid. If everyone in the group follows this system, then people can eat a variety of hot dinners, none of which need cooking. The most efficient bowl is a hard, two- to three-cup plastic container with a screw-on lid; it can also serve as a container for rehydrating the next day's lunch. My favorite, though, is a deep, worn wooden bowl and a plastic bag, with a piece of tin foil or whatever I can find to serve as a temporary lid while "cooking." If you carefully lick your bowl, spoon, and army knife (across the fairly dull blade) and add a bit of boiling water when you're done, there is absolutely no clean-up involved.

In the desert, I've found that—in addition to lots and lots of water and some salt—fresh, tangy, or wet foods are especially welcome. Hard cheeses such as Parmesan last surprisingly well if tucked deep into the middle of your pack away from the sun's penetrating warmth. I hang fresh parsley on the outside of my pack; it will eventually dry. A bag of bulky, delicate, and salty popcorn or pretzels can also be stored outside your pack in this climate.

Favorite recipes: See Sanna's Wheat Salad on page 80, Scrambled Sushi Dinner on page 127, and Mashed Potato Dinner on page 120.

CAKES AND MUFFINS ·············

As I experimented with steamed puddings, I discovered that some box mixes for cakes and muffins actually "bake" fairly well in an oven bag. This method is quite handy for one or two people because, as with steamed puddings, you need no baking device at all, and there are also no dirty pots to clean.

Date Muffins

For a treat that's quick in preparation at home and on trail, try these Date Muffins in a bag. For variations, try blueberry muffin, raspberry muffin, banana nut muffin, and other muffin mixes.

At home, combine in a small oven bag:
- ¾ cup date muffin mix (about half of a 9-ounce mix)
- 2 teaspoons powdered eggs
- 1 tablespoon powdered milk

On trail, add:
- ¼ cup water

to bag and mix ingredients well. Cook for 10 minutes, following directions on page 141.

Servings: Each bag makes one roundish muffin about 1¼ inch high and 5¼ inches in diameter. Serves one or two.

Nutritional information: 460 calories, 13 grams fat, 76 grams carbohydrate, and 9 grams protein per recipe.

©Ben Townsend

▲ ▲ ▲

High-altitude Baking

As altitude goes up, leavening agents like baking powder and baking soda become more potent, making air pockets in the batter larger than they would be at lower altitudes. Larger air pockets mean thinner walls, which in turn can cause a cake to fall. A rise in altitude also increases evaporation, which makes the cake dry.

To counteract these effects, it is necessary to adjust the ingredients. Because it is impossible to reduce the amount of baking powder in a commercial mix, cake mix manufacturers direct users to add 4 tablespoons flour for every 3 cups cake mix when above 3,500 feet. (For 1 cup cake mix, add 1 tablespoon plus 1 teaspoon flour.)

The makers of one convection-type trail oven recommend adding 3 tablespoons flour and 3 tablespoons water for every 2 cups commercial cake mix when above 5,000 feet. If you are making cakes from scratch, also decrease the baking powder by ½ teaspoon at 5,000 feet, another ½ teaspoon at 7,500 feet, and so on. (For 1 cup commercial cake mix, add 1½ tablespoons flour and 1½ tablespoons water. When baking from scratch, also decrease baking powder by ¼ teaspoon at 5,000 feet and every increment of 2,500 feet thereafter.)

Because evaporation is not a problem when using boil-in-a-bag type trail bakers and the liquid/flour balance is tightly prescribed, makers of these devices simply recommend increasing the cooking time 1 minute for every 2,000 feet of gain in elevation.

Cookbooks on the topic of high-altitude baking give more complicated instructions involving decreasing the baking powder or baking soda and sugar, increasing the liquid and flour, and increasing the oven temperature.

I have not tested these recipes at altitude. If I were headed to the high country with a baking device, I'd follow the manufacturer's advice. For one- or two-person recipes that are made without a device, I'd follow the instructions above for boil-in-a-bag bakers.

Yellow Cake

I experimented with several commercial cake mixes using the boil-in-a-bag technique, and the cakes turned out fine except when I used Jiffy cake mixes. I have read that Jiffy cake mixes (though otherwise excellent) do not respond well to powdered eggs, which would account for my frustration when using this brand.

For a variation, use chocolate cake mix instead of yellow cake mix and for true decadence, toss 2 tablespoons chocolate chips into the dry mix.

At home, combine in a small oven bag:

1 cup yellow cake mix
1 tablespoon powdered eggs

Mix well and close with tie. Store in refrigerator or freezer.

On trail, add:

¼ cup water

and mix well. Cook 10 minutes according to directions on page 141.

Servings: Makes a small cake 5¼ inches in diameter by 1¼ inches high (or, half of a one-layer cake). Serves one or two.
Nutritional information: 641 calories, 18 grams fat, 117 grams carbohydrate, and 9 grams protein per recipe.

Variation: Poppy Seed Cake

To the cake mix, add:

1 tablespoon whole poppy seeds
¼ teaspoon dried lemon peel (optional)

Nutritional information: 686 calories, 22 grams fat, 119 grams carbohydrate, and 11 grams protein per recipe.

Variation: **Pecan Apricot Cake**

To the cake mix, add:

    1 tablespoon minced dried apricot
    2 tablespoons chopped pecans

Nutritional information: 799 calories, 29 grams fat, 131 grams carbohydrate, and 12 grams protein per recipe.

Variation: **Raisin-Nut Cake**

To the cake mix, add:

    ⅛ teaspoon cinnamon
    ⅛ teaspoon ground cloves
    1/16 teaspoon nutmeg
    2 tablespoons chopped nuts (your choice)
    1 teaspoon wheat germ
    1 tablespoon raisins

Nutritional information: 773 calories, 28 grams fat, 130 grams carbohydrate, and 13 grams protein per recipe.

Variation: **Carrot Cake**

Carrot flakes are slightly thinner than sliced carrots so the flakes work better here. Ideally, the flakes should be rehydrated on trail and then added to the other ingredients, but in practice it's a lot easier to pack all the ingredients together, add water, and bake. The carrots may come out a little chewy, but not enough to make a difference in the texture.

    To the cake mix, add:
    ⅛ teaspoon cinnamon
    ⅛ teaspoon ground cloves
    1/16 teaspoon nutmeg
    1 tablespoon nuts
    1 teaspoon wheat germ
    1 tablespoon dried carrot flakes

Nutritional information: 703 calories, 23 grams fat, 121 grams carbohydrate, and 10 grams protein per recipe.

MAKING CAKE WITH TRAIL BAKERS

For cakes that will serve three or four, use one of the baking devices discussed in Chapter 2 and follow the directions given below. **Note:** If you add fruit or nuts to recipes cooked in a backpacking Dutch oven or a convection-oven type baker, the cake may take a few minutes longer to bake.

Backpacking Dutch oven (7 inches in diameter): The pan should be filled no more than half full because the batter will rise too near the lid, thus burning the upper crust. Be sure to grease the pan. Use:

> **1 cup cake mix**
> **1 tablespoon powdered eggs**
> **½ cup minus 1 tablespoon water**

Bake 15 minutes or until done. Makes three or four servings.

Boil-in-a-bag type baker (5½ inches in diameter): If you add nuts or dried or fresh fruit, increase baking time 3 to 5 minutes. Use:

> **1 cup cake mix**
> **1 tablespoon powdered eggs**
> **½ cup water**

Bake/boil 12 minutes and let stand 3 minutes. Makes two servings.

If you use ¾ cup cake mix, adjust the eggs and water accordingly, boil/bake 8 to 10 minutes, and let stand 3 minutes. Makes one to two servings.

If you use 1½ cups cake mix, adjust the other ingredients accordingly, boil/bake 15 to 18 minutes, and let stand 5 minutes. Makes two to three servings.

Boil-in-a-bag type baker (7½ inches in diameter): If adding nuts or dried or fresh fruit, increase baking time 3 to 5 minutes. Use:

> **2 cups cake mix**
> **2 tablespoons powdered eggs**
> **1 cup water**

Boil/bake 20 minutes and let stand 5 minutes. Makes three or four servings.

If you use ¾ cup cake mix, adjust the other ingredients accordingly, boil/bake 8 to 10 minutes, and let stand 3 minutes. Makes one to two servings.

If you use 1½ cups cake mix, adjust the other ingredients accordingly, boil/bake 15 to 18 minutes, and let stand 5 minutes. Makes two to three servings.

If you use 3 cups cake mix, adjust the other ingredients accordingly, boil/bake 22 to 26 minutes, and let stand 5 minutes. Makes four to six servings.

Convection-oven type baker: Use a quick-release sheet (available as an accessory) or grease pan well to prevent cake from sticking.
For a 6-inch diameter pan use:
  ¾ cup cake mix
  2 teaspoons powdered eggs
  ¼ cup plus 1 tablespoon water
Bake for 15 minutes. Makes one to two servings.
For a 7-inch diameter pan use:
  1 cup cake mix
  1 tablespoon powdered eggs
  ½ cup minus 1 tablespoon water
Bake 15 minutes. Makes two servings.
For an 8-inch diameter pan use:
  1½ cups cake mix
  1 tablespoon plus 1 teaspoon powdered eggs
  ½ cup plus 2 tablespoons water
Bake 15 minutes or until done. Makes three or four servings.

Convection-oven type baker that comes with a non-stick pan 8 inches in diameter: This pan flares slightly, so it can hold more cake mix than a regular 8-inch pot. Combine:
  2 cups cake mix
  2 tablespoons powdered eggs
  ¾ cup plus 1 tablespoon water
Bake 15 to 20 minutes or until done. Makes four servings.

PIES •••••••••••••••••••••••••••

For a special dessert, take along a large graham cracker pie crust or individual pie crusts. You can find both in the baking section of your supermarket. The small crusts carry better and are less likely to break into pieces en route, but the large crust is nice for the effect—an actual pie on trail. Even if the crust cracks, the plastic cover more or less holds the pieces in place and your piece is going to get mushed when you transfer it to your bowl, anyway. (As an alternative, you can use individual sponge cakes. These are crushable—so they must be packed carefully—and have a shorter pack life.)

An 8-inch pie crust, which weighs almost 8 ounces (with packaging), holds 2 to 3½ cups of filling and makes four huge, six moderate, or eight small servings. The individual crusts, which weigh almost an ounce each (with packaging), hold ⅓ cup filling. Unless you are partial to the idea that less is better, consider taking two small crusts per person. Assuming that two hikers would be more likely to use these recipes, both pie recipes presented here will serve two.

If you are weight-conscious, then skip the crust with its aluminum pie plate and carry along some crumbled graham crackers and sprinkle the pieces over the filling.

You can, of course, fill the pie shell with your favorite pudding/fruit combo, or pair up other ingredients that naturally go together like chocolate pudding and dried cherries (Black Forest Pie), chocolate pudding and coffee (Mocha Pie), or coconut pudding and dried bananas (Coconut-Banana Pie).

For an elegant dessert, use one package instant pudding in a graham cracker crust and decorate with dried fruit.

Piña Colada Pie*

On trail, it is hard to get the pudding to mix evenly if you have already added the pineapple; instead, make the pudding, let it stand, and then add the fruit.

On trail, add:

> 1 cup cold water

to the pudding mix, stir thoroughly, and let stand 5 minutes. Add the pineapple. Serve in the pie crusts.

Servings: Makes two servings of 2 small pies each.
Nutritional information: 403 calories, 14 grams fat, 63 grams carbohydrate, and 6 grams protein per serving.

At home, put in a plastic bag and tie off:

¼ cup plus 2 tablespoons chopped dried pineapple

Then add:

⅓ cup powdered milk
¼ cup instant coconut pudding mix

Also pack:

4 small graham cracker crusts

Creamy Peach Pie*

In this recipe vanilla pudding holds everything together, but the flavor of peaches and spices is dominant. Soaking the peaches softens them and brings out their flavor. Nutmeg is potent so use it sparingly.

On trail, place peaches in an insulated container and add 1 cup boiling water. Cover and let stand 10 minutes. Cool. Gradually add pudding mix, stirring thoroughly. Serve in the pie crusts.

Servings: Makes two servings of 2 small pies each.
Nutritional information: 466 calories, 13 grams fat, 79 grams carbohydrate, and 8 grams protein per serving.

At home, put in a plastic bag and tie off:

⅓ cup powdered milk
¼ cup instant vanilla pudding mix
1 teaspoon vanilla powder
1 teaspoon butter powder
2 pinches cinnamon
1 pinch nutmeg

Then add:

¼ cup plus 2 tablespoons chopped dried peaches

Also pack:

4 small graham cracker crusts

OTHER DESSERTS ・・・・・・・・・・・・・・

John's Fruit Crisp

John Emelin reports that the first time he tried this dish, he forgot the butter or margarine, so on trail he just squirted some olive oil in with the flour/sugar mixture to bind the ingredients together, and it turned out fine.

On trail, lightly grease the pot. Add the fruit, add water to cover, and allow to rehydrate for 20 minutes or simmer over low heat to promote rehydration.

In the meantime, empty the envelope of dessert topping and the powdered milk into a water bottle and add ½ cup water. Put the cap on the bottle and shake it. Keep shaking until contents reach the consistency of whipped cream.

Add the butter, margarine, or oil to the flour mix (cut the margarine or butter into small chunks and mix it around) and sprinkle this mixture over the top of the fruit. Cover tightly and simmer. The fruit should have enough water to moisten the flour mixture as it settles on the fruit. If it seems too dry as it cooks, add a little water. The crisp is done when the topping looks cooked and is, well, crisp on top. Serve with whipped topping.

Servings: Using 3 cups fruit, makes approximately four servings of ⅔ cup each.

Nutritional information: Using 2½ cups dried peaches, 552 calories, 13 grams fat, 97 grams carbohydrate, and 7 grams protein; using 2½ cups dried apples, 577 calories, 13 grams fat, 104 grams carbohydrate, and 4 grams protein.

■

At home, pack:

2 to 3 cups dried peaches, raspberries, strawberries, blueberries, or apples

Pack separately:

2 tablespoons flour
2 tablespoons oatmeal
¼ cup white sugar
¼ cup brown sugar
¼ teaspoon nutmeg
¼ teaspoon cinnamon

Pack separately:

envelope of whipped dessert topping
2 to 3 tablespoons powdered milk

Also carry:

3 to 4 tablespoons butter, margarine or vegetable oil

Chunky Applesauce*

Applesauce is good as a side dish for dinner, as dessert, and as a topping for regular pancakes or potato pancakes. This instant version is super easy. The potato starch thickens the applesauce liquid and gives it a nice texture, but you can omit this ingredient if it is not on hand. You can also make this recipe with dried pears or dried peaches, or a combination of several kinds of dried fruit.

On trail, place ingredients in an insulated bowl or mug and add:
  ½ cup boiling water
Cover and let stand 10 minutes.

Servings: Makes one serving of ½ cup.
Nutritional information: 90 calories, 0 grams fat, 22 grams carbohydrate, and 0 grams protein.

At home, chop into very small pieces in a blender:
4 dried apple rings (about ¼ cup)

Place apple bits in a plastic bag, add the following ingredients, and mix well:
1 teaspoon brown sugar
pinch cinnamon
½ teaspoon potato starch

Variation: Piña Colada Applesauce*

Use 1 tablespoon plus 1 teaspoon powdered piña colada mix instead of the brown sugar, cinnamon, and potato starch.

Nutritional information: 123 calories, 0 grams fat, 30 grams carbohydrate, and 0 grams protein.

Some More S'mores*

Ever tried to make s'mores on a stove? Of course not. S'mores need the open flame of a wood fire, or the heat of charcoal, to melt the marshmallows and chocolate into a gooey graham cracker sandwich. But if you love s'mores, don't despair. This recipe combines two of the key ingredients with toasted nuts to make a downright luscious dessert.

No need to worry about the graham crackers crumbling in your pack—they are crumbled already, but still provide a satisfying crunch. Chocolate is the predominant flavor, while the toasted walnuts add a little more "mouthfeel." (Yes, you could just pack along a chocolate bar with some crunchy ingredient, but think of all the cooking points you gain by making this impressive dessert on trail.) This dessert is very rich, so half a recipe per person may be enough.

To crumble the graham crackers, place in a bowl and crush with the bottom of a sturdy glass.

It's a little messy getting the dessert out of the plastic bag, but anyone who's a pot-licker will love having a backcountry "pot" to lick.

At home, combine in a small oven bag:

1½ **crumbled graham crackers (½ cup)**
¼ **cup chocolate chips**
¼ **cup chopped, toasted walnuts**

On trail, make sure the bag is securely tied shut and drop it in hot water until the chocolate has melted. Remove from water and spoon contents into bowl.

Servings: Makes one serving of 1 cup or two servings of ½ cup each.
Nutritional information: 449 calories, 32 grams fat, 44 grams carbohydrate, and 9 grams protein per recipe.

Alan Kesselheim's Hot Tips

Alan, author of *The Lightweight Gourmet: Drying and Cooking Food for the Outdoor Life* and other books, writes frequently for *BACKPACKER*. He and his wife have twice paddled across Canada on fourteen-month trips that included wintering over in the Far North.

Style: I guess I'm a gourmand, since I favor variety, pleasure, and some amount of organization. I'm not one to slave over meal preparation or take along all manner of kitchen gadgetry, however. My preference is to achieve these goals as simply as possible, and by handling much of the work before leaving town.

Standbys: I'm a fan of hot breakfasts, although I like the speed and economy of cold cereal. Lunch is tough, especially if you aren't a big fan of PB&J. One way to add variety and spice to lunch is to take along hummus. You can carry it dry and rehydrate it in the field, or carry it wet for the first day. (Also see Alan's Spicy Teriyaki Turkey Jerky, page 82.)

One of my favorite backpackable dinners is pesto with noodles. If you make your own pesto, combine all the ingredients except the oil or melted butter and blend them in a food processor until they are a thick paste. You may need to add a little water. Spread the paste on a tray, dry at 125 degrees, cool, then pulverize in a blender to get a powder. On trail, add the butter or oil slowly.

Gadget: I consider two gadgets indispensable: the dehydrator, which has revolutionized my outdoor life and allowed me and my family to go long, go cheap, and go nutritious; and a good coffee filter that does away with messy paper or cloth inserts. Several one-cup filters that don't need inserts are available.

Trail wisdom: Take a really complete spice kit and a few personal favorite condiments— soy sauce with hot pepper flavoring, Tabasco, gourmet mustard, some Parmesan, whatever.

APPENDIX A

Where to Find Ingredients

This appendix will help you locate sources for some of the freeze-dried, dried, and specialty foods mentioned in this book. It is divided into two parts. The first section is an alphabetical list of ingredients, each of which is followed by the name of the supplier/s (or other source) and the typical quantities available. The second section provides addresses and other information about the suppliers.

The ingredients listing is not exhaustive. In general, pre-mixed dishes (such as green beans with onions, tomatoes, and sliced almonds) are not included, although products of special interest, such as pre-mixed salads, eggroll filling, and salsa are included. When the source is supermarkets or health food stores, a brand name is not generally given because there may be several brands, any of which can be used in the recipes.

Information regarding ounces per package, measure once rehydrated, and number of servings is from the suppliers. Information concerning dry measure is from the author.

Suppliers may change their offerings. For current mail-order catalogs, contact the suppliers.

Note: Information from the Internet Grocer was received too late to integrate into the following list of ingredients. See page 164 for more about the Internet Grocer.

INGREDIENTS

Almond paste: Gourmet food stores; supermarkets (generally 7 ounces); The Baker's Catalogue (16 ounces)

Apple flakes: AlpineAire (8 ounces, which makes 2 cups)

Apples, diced: AlpineAire (8 ounces, which makes 2 cups)

Asparagus, diced freeze-dried: Adventure Foods (0.5 ounces, which serves two); AlpineAire (2 ounces, which makes 2 cups)

Bacon bits, pre-fried: Supermarkets (various, usually about 3 ounces)

Bacon strips, pre-fried: Supermarkets

Beans, dried flakes and powdered: Health food stores; supermarkets

Beans, cooked freeze-dried: Adventure Foods, including black and kidney beans (8 ounces); Adventure Foods, refried pinto beans (6 ounces, which serves two); AlpineAire, including pinto, small white, black, and kidney beans (16 ounces, which makes 8 cups); Backpacker's Pantry, refried beans (no amount given, serves two)

Beans, green, freeze-dried: Richmoor (0.38 ounce, which serves two; 0.75 ounce, which serves four)

Beef, cooked dried: Supermarkets (amount varies, but generally is 4 to 5 ounces)

Beef, cooked freeze-dried: Adventure Foods, freeze-dried ground (2.2 ounces); AlpineAire, diced (1 ounce, which makes $\frac{2}{3}$ cup; 8 ounces, which makes $5\frac{1}{3}$ cups); Backpacker's Pantry (1 ounce); Richmoor (1 ounce)

Beef, dried: *See* Jerky

Beef spread: Adventure Foods (two- and four-person servings)

Bell peppers, sweet dried mixed red and green: AlpineAire (4 ounces, which makes 4 cups); health food stores (bulk)

Blueberries, whole freeze-dried: AlpineAire (1 ounce, which serves two; 4 ounces, number served varies)

Bouillon powder: Health food stores; supermarkets

Bread bases: Supermarkets; The Baker's Catalogue (16 ounces, enough for about two dozen pizzas)

Broccoli, freeze-dried: Adventure Foods (0.6 ounces, which serves two); AlpineAire, chopped (2 ounces, which makes 4 cups)

Butter-flavored sprinkles: Supermarkets (2 to 2.5 ounces)

Butter powder: The Baker's Catalogue (8 ounces, about $2\frac{2}{3}$ cups powder)

Buttermilk powder: Supermarkets (16 ounces, about 4 cups powder, which makes about 16 cups buttermilk); The Baker's Catalogue (16 ounces)

Cabbage, diced dried: AlpineAire (8 ounces, which makes $5\frac{1}{2}$ cups)

Carrots, dried: Adventure Foods (2 ounces, which serves two); AlpineAire (16 ounces, which makes $10\frac{1}{2}$ cups)

Celery, cross-cut dried: AlpineAire (4 ounces, which makes 7 cups)

Cheese powder: AlpineAire, cheddar (2 ounces, which makes ½ cup and serves two; 8 ounces, which makes 2 cups and serves four); Cabot Annex Store; supermarkets that carry Cabot cheese; The Baker's Catalogue, orange and white cheddar (8 ounces, which equals about 2⅔ cups dry measure)

Cheese powder, blue: The Baker's Catalogue (8 ounces, which equals about 2⅔ cups dry measure)

Chicken, cooked freeze-dried: AlpineAire (1 ounce, which makes ⅔ cup; 8 ounces, which makes 5⅓ cups); Backpacker's Pantry (1 ounce); Richmoor (1 ounce)

Chicken salad, freeze-dried mix: Adventure Foods (5.3 ounces, which serves two; 10.1 ounces, which serves four)

Cider, powdered: Supermarkets

Coconut, powdered: The Baker's Catalogue (8 ounces)

Coconut cream powder: Asian food stores (1.75 ounces, which is about ½ cup powder)

Corn, freeze-dried: Adventure Foods (1.6 ounces, which serves two); AlpineAire (1.5 ounces, which serves two; 8 ounces, which makes 5½ cups); Backpacker's Pantry (1.5 ounces, which serves two; 3 ounces, which serves four); Richmoor (1 ounce, which serves two; 2 ounces, which serves four)

Couscous: AlpineAire, (16 ounces, which makes 5⅓ cups); supermarkets and health food stores (10- to 12-ounce boxes)

Couscous, whole wheat: AlpineAire (16 ounces, which makes 8 cups); supermarkets and health food stores (10- to 12-ounce boxes)

Crab salad, freeze-dried mix: Adventure Foods, with whitefish (5.3 ounces, which serves two; 11 ounces, which serves four)

Crab spread, deviled: Adventure Foods (packaged for two and four servings)

Eggroll filling: Adventure Foods (fills 16 wrappers)

Egg replacer: Health food stores; some supermarkets

Eggs, dried whole (powdered eggs): Adventure Foods (2 ounces, which makes 4 eggs); AlpineAire (12 ounces, which makes 24 eggs); some health food stores; The Baker's Catalogue (8 ounces)

Fruit, dried, various: Baking, gourmet, and outdoor food catalogs; health food stores; supermarkets

Garlic, dried, powdered, or diced: Health food stores (bulk); supermarkets

Ginger, candied: Health food stores (bulk); supermarkets (approximately 3 ounces); The Baker's Catalogue (16 ounces)

Ginger, ground: Health food stores; supermarkets

Ginger, dried pieces: Health food stores

Gravy, beef- and chicken-flavored: Supermarkets

Jerky: Adventure Foods, meatless Cajun style (16 ounces); Backpacker's Pantry, beef (1.1 ounces); supermarkets (various amounts)

Lentils, cooked freeze-dried: Adventure Foods (8 ounces); AlpineAire (16 ounces, which makes 8 cups)

Macaroni: See Pasta

Maple syrup granules: Adventure Foods (2.6 ounces, which serves one); AlpineAire (8 ounces, which makes 1¾ cups); Richmoor (6.25 ounces, which makes 2 cups)

Meat substitutes: Adventure Foods, beef style, Canadian bacon flavor, and chicken style (8 ounces)

Mushrooms, dried: AlpineAire (1 ounce, which serves two as side dish; 4 ounces, which makes 4 cups); Asian food stores; health food stores; supermarkets

Onions, chopped dried: AlpineAire (8 ounces, which makes 5½ cups); health food stores (bulk); supermarkets (small containers)

Orange-flavored breakfast powder: Supermarkets

Orange powder: The Baker's Catalogue (8 ounces, which equals about 1½ cups dry measure)

Pasta, no-cook (no-boil): AlpineAire, instant vegetable spirals and instant whole wheat macaroni (8 ounces, which makes 6 cups)

Pasta, regular, whole wheat, and vegetable-flavored: Health food stores; supermarkets

Pasta salad: Adventure Foods, with vegetables (11.5 ounces, which serves two; 23 ounces, which serves four); AlpineAire, rainbow garden (3 ounces, which serves two as side dish)

Peaches, freeze-dried: AlpineAire, diced (0.75 ounces, which serves two)

Peas, freeze-dried: Adventure Foods (1.9 ounces, which serves two); AlpineAire (1.5 ounces, which serves two; 8 ounces, which makes 5½ cups); Backpacker's Pantry (1.5 ounces, which serves two; 3 ounces, which serves four); Backpacker's Pantry (1.37 ounces and 2.75 ounces); Richmoor (1 ounce, which serves two; 2 ounces, which serves four)

Pineapple, freeze-dried pieces: AlpineAire (0.75 ounce, which serves two)

Potato starch: Asian food stores (16 ounces); gourmet shops; The Baker's Catalogue (16 ounces, which equals approximately 3 cups dry measure)

Potatoes, freeze-dried diced: AlpineAire (4 ounces, which makes 3 cups)

Potatoes, instant hash browns: Supermarkets (6 ounces, which makes approximately 2¼ cups)

Potatoes, instant mashed: AlpineAire (3.5 ounces, which serves two as side dish; 16 ounces, which makes 16 cups); health food stores; supermarkets

Rice, brown, cooked and dehydrated: Adventure Foods (8 ounces)

Rice, brown, cooked freeze-dried: AlpineAire (2 ounces, which serves two as side dish; 8 ounces, which makes 4 cups)

Rice, white, instant: AlpineAire (16 ounces, which makes 8 cups); supermarkets

Rice, wild, cooked and dried: Gibbs Wild Rice (4 ounces)

Rice, wild, instant: AlpineAire (8 ounces, which makes 4 cups)

Salsa, dried: Some health food stores

Shortening, powdered vegetable: Harvest Foodworks (3.5 ounces, which equals 10 tablespoons dry measure and is equivalent to 20 tablespoons shortening)

Shrimp, freeze-dried: AlpineAire (4 ounces, which makes 2 cups)

Sour cream powder: AlpineAire (8 ounces, which makes 2 cups); The Baker's Catalogue (8 ounces)

Spinach powder: The Baker's Catalogue (8 ounces, which equals about 2¼ cups dry measure)

Strawberries, freeze-dried: AlpineAire, whole (1 ounce, which serves two; 4 ounces, amount varies)

Tomato bits: Sonoma brand from Timber Crest Farms (4 ounces); Sonoma brand from Timber Crest Farms, tomato bits with seasoning (4.75 ounces)

Tomato flakes: The Baker's Catalogue (8 ounces, which equals 5½ cups)

Tomato powder: Adventure Foods (4 ounces); AlpineAire (2 ounces; 8 ounces, which makes 6 cups sauce and serves twelve); The Baker's Catalogue (8 ounces, which equals about 1¼ cups plus 1 tablespoon dry measure)

Tomatoes, dried: AlpineAire, diced (4 ounces, which makes 4 cups); supermarkets; The Baker's Catalogue (8 ounces); Sonoma brand from Timber Crest Farms

Tuna, freeze-dried: AlpineAire (4 ounces, which makes 2 cups)

Tuna salad, freeze-dried mix: Adventure Foods (5 ounces, which serves two; 10.4 ounces, which serves four)

Turkey, freeze-dried: AlpineAire (1 ounce, which makes ⅔ cup; 8 ounces, which makes 5⅓ cups); Backpacker's Pantry (1 ounce)

Vanilla powder: The Baker's Catalogue (2 ounces, which equals about ½ cup dry measure)

Vegetable toppings, roasted: The Baker's Catalogue, includes tomato, garlic, chili, onion, red bell pepper toppings (4 ounces each)

Vegetables, mixed dried: AlpineAire, Garden Vegetables including dried carrots, freeze-dried peas and corn (1.5 ounces, which serves two; 3 ounces, which serves four; 8 ounces, which makes 5½ cups); AlpineAire, Vegetable Mix including dried carrots, onions, celery, and red and green peppers along with freeze-dried peas (1.5 ounces, which serves two; 3 ounces, which serves four; 8 ounces, which makes 5½ cups); Just Veggies, dried carrots, bell peppers, and tomatoes with freeze-dried corn and peas (various amounts from 1 to 8 ounces); Sonoma brand from Timber Crest Farms, Toss-Ta including dried julienne tomatoes, onion, mushroom, garlic, spinach, shallot, jalapeño, celery, bell pepper, and spices (3 ounces)

Health food stores often have a mix that includes dried peas, potatoes, and/or carrots that does not rehydrate rapidly. Many supermarkets carry dried vegetable mixes that can be added to soups or stews, but these also include dried vegetables that do not rehydrate rapidly.

Wasabi: Asian markets; health food stores (2.5 ounces, which equals a little more than ¾ cup dry measure); supermarkets

Za'atar: The Baker's Catalogue (8 ounces)

SOURCES

Adventure Foods: For mail order, 481 Banjo Road, Whittier, NC 28789; (704) 497-4113.

AlpineAire: For mail order, P.O. Box 1600, Nevada City, CA 95959; (800) 322-6325.

Backpacker's Pantry: For a list of local suppliers, 6350 Gunpark Drive, Boulder, CO 80301; (303) 581-0518.

The Baker's Catalogue: For mail order, P.O. Box 876, Norwich, VT 05055-0876; (800) 827-6836.

Cabot Annex Store: For mail order, Route 100, Waterbury, VT 05676; (802) 244-6334. Store representatives will also provide the names of local stores that carry Cabot products.

Gibbs Wild Rice: For mail order, P.O. Box 277, Deer River, MN 56636; (800) 344-6378.

Harvest Foodworks: 66 Victoria Avenue, Smiths Falls, Ontario, Canada K7A 2P4; (800) 268-4268. Harvest Foodworks does not sell mail order to individual customers, but Piragis Northwoods Company carries Harvest Foodworks products and does sell by mail order through The Boundary Waters Catalog, 105 North Central Avenue, Ely, MN 55731; (800) 223-6565.

The Internet Grocer: The Internet Grocer sells many freeze-dried and dehydrated foods—including interesting items like strawberry-apple flakes, taco-flavored textured vegetable protein, and peanut butter powder—but in bulk only. A #2½ can, which holds almost a quart, is the smallest unit. (Note that fruits and vegetables in #2½ cans are dehydrated, not freeze-dried.) Food is also available by #10 can, which holds almost a gallon; by the case; and by the 6-gallon "pail."

Although the larger amounts are suitable for trip programs, individuals can put together a coop order (see page 21 for ideas about putting together a backwoods food coop order.)

For more information, contact the Internet Grocer at http://www.internet-grocer.com or by mail or phone: 1713 Cascade Street, Mesquite, TX 75149; before 1:30 P.M. Central Time, (214) 742-777, and after 2:00 P.M. Central Time, (972) 288-0262.

Just Veggies: For mail order, Box 807, Westley, CA 95387; (800) 537-1985. Also available in health food stores.

Richmoor: For a list of local suppliers , P.O. Box 8092, Van Nuys CA, 91409; (818) 787-2010.

Sonoma products from Timber Crest Farms: For a list of local suppliers, Timber Crest Farms, 4791 Dry Creek Road, Healdsburg, CA 95448; (707) 433-8251.

APPENDIX B

Backcountry Baking and Cooking Devices

The BakePacker is available at outdoor stores. It is made by Strike 2 Industries, 508 E. Augusta Avenue, Spokane, WA 99207; (509) 484-3701. *The Bakepacker's Companion* by Jean S. Spangenberg is available through Adventure Foods (see Appendix A, Sources).

The Banks Fry-Bake Oven and pot tongs are available from Banks Fry-Bake Company, P.O. Box 183, Claverack, NY 12513; (518) 851-5207 or (888) 379-2253.

The MSR heat exchanger is available at outdoor stores. It is made by Mountain Safety Research, P.O. Box 24547, Seattle, WA, 98124; (800) 877-9677 or (206) 624-8573.

The OutBack Oven and accessories are available at outdoor stores. They are made by Cascade Designs, 4000 First Avenue S., Seattle, WA 98134; (206) 583-0583.

INDEX

About the Author

An outdoor expert who loves to eat well in the backcountry, Dorcas Miller is the author of nine books, including *Good Food for Camp and Trail* and *Stars of the First People: Native American Star Myths and Constellations*. She has written for several outdoor magazines and is a frequent contributor to *BACKPACKER*. She lives in Chelsea, Maine.

The mission of *BACKPACKER* magazine is to distribute, in a variety of media, credible, in-depth, and compelling "how-to-do-it" information about wilderness recreation, primarily in North America.

BACKPACKER magazine
33 East Minor Street
Emmaus, PA 18098
Phone: 1-610-967-5171
fax: 1-610-967-8181
web address: www.bpbasecamp.com

Founded in 1906, The Mountaineers is a Seattle-based non-profit outdoor activity and conservation club with 15,000 members, whose mission is "to explore, study, preserve, and enjoy the natural beauty of the outdoors . . . . " The club sponsors many classes and year-round outdoor activities in the Pacific Northwest, and supports environmental causes by sponsoring legislation and presenting educational programs. The Mountaineers Books supports the club's mission by publishing travel and natural history guides, instructional texts, and works on conservation and history. For information, call or write The Mountaineers, Club Headquarters, 300 Third Avenue West, Seattle, Washington, 98119; (206) 284-6310.

Send or call for our catalog of more than 300 outdoor titles:

The Mountaineers Books
1001 SW Klickitat Way, Suite 201
Seattle, WA 98134
1-800-553-4453
e-mail: mbooks@mountaineers.org
website: www.mountaineers.org